C000274195

'Finally! Someone has broken
of Digital Marketing! I hope
book to first year marketing
everyone who is currently in
that digital marketing is not
be sharing it far and wide.'

Tara Hunt, *digital marketing agency owner, social media*
pioneer, and author of The Whuffie Factor

'I found this book equal parts enjoyable and useful. It
comfortably traverses altitudes between the higher-level
strategic concepts that underpin everything marketers do for
brands, while providing real, actionable data and advice for
someone looking to have a successful career in the field. This
guide is as useful to an experienced marketer wanting to learn
about new tools and develop new ways of approaching their
work as it is for someone considering becoming a marketer
as they enter the workforce or make a career change. That
versatility and easy voice made it a pleasure to read, and
the insights in the book made it a useful learning tool for
marketers at any level.'

Adam Sohn, *Vice President Communications,*
Lockheed Martin Space

'A handy companion book for anyone looking to gain a
marketing qualification or embark upon a successful career in
marketing in our digital age. Our fast-evolving industry needs
a constant stream of fresh talent to create tomorrow's winning
campaigns. With this book as your guide, the next great digital
marketer might be you.'

Allister Frost, *Founder and Managing Consultant,*
Wild Orange Media Ltd

'This title is a must read for those making the transition
between traditional marketing practices to digital marketing,
and those working with or managing digital marketers. It
provides great insight into the fast-paced environment and the
terms used in the day to day life of a digital marketer, as well
as key formulas required to deliver an analytical approach to
this discipline. You'll get an excellent foundation of knowledge
from this book.'

Jemma Davis, *JeMarketing, Freelance Marketing Expert*

DIGITAL MARKETER

BCS, THE CHARTERED INSTITUTE FOR IT

BCS, The Chartered Institute for IT, is committed to making IT good for society. We use the power of our network to bring about positive, tangible change. We champion the global IT profession and the interests of individuals, engaged in that profession, for the benefit of all.

Exchanging IT expertise and knowledge

The Institute fosters links between experts from industry, academia and business to promote new thinking, education and knowledge sharing.

Supporting practitioners

Through continuing professional development and a series of respected IT qualifications, the Institute seeks to promote professional practice tuned to the demands of business. It provides practical support and information services to its members and volunteer communities around the world.

Setting standards and frameworks

The Institute collaborates with government, industry and relevant bodies to establish good working practices, codes of conduct, skills frameworks and common standards. It also offers a range of consultancy services to employers to help them adopt best practice.

Become a member

Over 70,000 people including students, teachers, professionals and practitioners enjoy the benefits of BCS membership. These include access to an international community, invitations to a roster of local and national events, career development tools and a quarterly thought-leadership magazine. Visit www.bcs.org/membership to find out more.

Further Information
BCS, The Chartered Institute for IT,
First Floor, Block D,
North Star House, North Star Avenue,
Swindon, SN2 1FA, UK.
T +44 (0) 1793 417424
(Monday to Friday, 9.00 a.m. to 5.00 p.m. UK time)
www.bcs.org/contact

http://shop.bcs.org/

DIGITAL MARKETER

Eileen Brown and Betsy Aoki

bcs

The
Chartered
Institute
for IT

© 2018 BCS Learning & Development Ltd

Reprinted November 2018

The right of Eileen Brown and Betsy Aoki to be identified as authors of this work has been asserted by them in accordance with sections 77 and 78 of the Copyright, Designs and Patents Act 1988.

All rights reserved. Apart from any fair dealing for the purposes of research or private study, or criticism or review, as permitted by the Copyright Designs and Patents Act 1988, no part of this publication may be reproduced, stored or transmitted in any form or by any means, except with the prior permission in writing of the publisher, or in the case of reprographic reproduction, in accordance with the terms of the licences issued by the Copyright Licensing Agency. Enquiries for permission to reproduce material outside those terms should be directed to the publisher.

All trade marks, registered names etc. acknowledged in this publication are the property of their respective owners. BCS and the BCS logo are the registered trade marks of the British Computer Society charity number 292786 (BCS).

Published by BCS Learning & Development Ltd, a wholly owned subsidiary of BCS, The Chartered Institute for IT, First Floor, Block D, North Star House, North Star Avenue, Swindon, SN2 1FA, UK.
www.bcs.org

ISBN: 978-1-78017-4006
PDF ISBN: 978-1-78017-4013
ePUB ISBN: 978-1-78017-4020
Kindle ISBN: 978-1-78017-4037

Ebook
available

British Cataloguing in Publication Data.
A CIP catalogue record for this book is available at the British Library.

Disclaimer:
The views expressed in this book are of the author(s) and do not necessarily reflect the views of the Institute or BCS Learning & Development Ltd except where explicitly stated as such. Although every care has been taken by the author(s) and BCS Learning & Development Ltd in the preparation of the publication, no warranty is given by the author(s) or BCS Learning & Development Ltd as publisher as to the accuracy or completeness of the information contained within it and neither the author(s) nor BCS Learning & Development Ltd shall be responsible or liable for any loss or damage whatsoever arising by virtue of such information or any instructions or advice contained within this publication or by any of the aforementioned.

BCS books are available at special quantity discounts to use as premiums and sale promotions, or for use in corporate training programmes. Please visit our Contact us page at www.bcs.org/contact

Publisher's acknowledgements
Reviewers: Jemma Davis and Karen Manning
Publisher: Ian Borthwick
Commissioning Editor: Rebecca Youé
Production Manager: Florence Leroy
Project Manager: Sunrise Setting Ltd
Cover work: Alex Wright
Picture credits: Shutterstock - wildestanimal
Typeset by Lapiz Digital Services, Chennai, India.
Printed by Hobbs the Printers Ltd, Totton, Hampshire, SO40 3WX

This book is for Steve, and Jason – who keep us dancing through the rain...

CONTENTS

LIST OF FIGURES AND TABLES

AUTHORS

Eileen Brown brings 10 years of experience as a small business proprietor, digital marketing consultant and speaker to companies including Cisco, Dell, HP, IBM and Microsoft. She delivers marketing engagements for large and small public and commercial organisations, and writes about social business, Internet of Things (IoT) and artificial intelligence (AI) for ZDNet.com. She wrote the best-selling book *Working the Crowd: Social Media Marketing for Business*, published by BCS.

Elizabeth (Betsy) Aoki has worked for more than 20 years in the United States, leading web technology product development. In 2009 Microsoft asked her to switch from engineering to marketing/public relations, and build the just-launching Bing search engine brand on Twitter, as well as tech evangelism programmes. She made a return trip to Bing engineering to do metrics platforms and a year-long Election 2016 initiative, then on to Hulu for more metrics platform work. At the time of writing she serves as lead producer for services and infrastructure at Bungie, an American video game developer.

PREFACE

If you have ever persuaded someone to try new food, then you are a marketer. If you have convinced them to watch a new genre of film, then you are a marketer. Could you convince someone that the hot new fitness wearable is well worth trying, get them to buy the wearable and persuade their friends to buy the device too? If you can do this, not only have you delivered a successful marketing campaign but you have success metrics to measure your activities and you have created an influencer for the product.

Digital marketing uses a similar technique. Online marketing has the potential to persuade potentially thousands of people to try the new food, watch the film or buy the fitness wearable. Fundamentally the processes are the same. You are persuading people to do what you want them to and ensuring that they like you in the process. If you are interested in exploring digital marketing opportunities then this is the book for you.

This book covers the many aspects involved in being a digital marketer; from planning to strategy, platforms to analytics, role types and professional development. It will also delve into the skills that are required as a digital marketer and how the digital marketing role takes different shapes at different companies. In some cases, at some organisations, the digital marketer needs to be a jack of all trades.

Before early career professionals and marketing graduates embark upon their digital marketing journey or start to plan their digital marketing strategy, we would suggest that they read this book to understand the myriad opportunities that are available to the aspiring digital marketer. From traditional outbound marketing, to taking advantage of the Internet of Things (IoT), the role of digital marketer has never been more creative, with scope for innovation and opportunities to utilise new technical developments. The possibilities for marketing are almost endless. The book will also cover and explore entry points to the digital marketing career.

If you come to this book already familiar with the traditional marketing principles of customer acquisition and engagement, taste making and influence, campaign and conversion – then digital marketing will be an expansion of your skills and expertise into the digital realm. And for some in hard-hitting sales-driven commercial sectors, it may be the only way to keep your job or rise within the marketing profession. In the digital age, marketers must stay abreast of digital developments in the field as competitors use these new channels and approaches to lure customers away from your service or product.

Many developments in digital marketing are built on social media, which has evolved into a fundamental requirement for web marketing through the rise of platforms such as Twitter, Facebook, Instagram, Pinterest – popular destinations for affinity groups, families, friends and potential customers to gather and share information.

Just as you might put a notice on a pub or supermarket notice board that you are looking to buy (or sell) a lawnmower, give away an old sofa or sell those old baby items that have been cluttering up the spare room, social media platforms offer spaces for people to exchange goods, recommend services and products to others, communicate and bond with one another. These social networks of people can also create momentum for products, just as word-of-mouth was often a small businessperson's best friend.

The other strength of social platforms is their ability to share content – and when that content goes viral, so too does its creator's underlying message. These social media moments have become more powerful than advertising and often much cheaper. Now, corporate brands find they must use the techniques of organic influence within social marketing channels to find and recruit customers into the fold.

Then of course there are websites specific to reviews and recommendations – Yelp, TripAdvisor, OpenTable, Amazon, Trustpilot, Rotten Tomatoes and Revue, to name a few.

Even if the digital marketer does not have a technology degree, they must familiarise themselves with the technology that underlies these new channels, to enable them to make the best use of them.

This book can help to support a corporate transition from traditional to digital marketing activities. It can help in enhancing existing marketing activities, even if digital marketing is already being used. It can enable you to maximise efficacy and reach of digital channels or social networks, and it can aid in improving customer relationships and interactions through digital media. Many small businesses will use digital as an entry into advertising and this book can be used as an aid for those taking their first digital steps before moving into more complex multi-channel approaches. It will also support digital marketers with examples of good practice, guidelines, industry standards and templates.

However, without an effective monitoring and reporting strategy in place, all the marketer's efforts might come to naught. We want to stress that you should fully explore and understand the assorted opportunities that are available. With measures in place to track, monitor and fully assess the digital effect, you will be sure of digital marketing success.

BOOK STRUCTURE

This book will try to encompass as many aspects of the digital marketing role as possible and will try to provide a balance between being too basic and too detailed.

Chapter 1, 'Overview of the Digital Marketing Field', discusses the differences and similarities between digital marketing and other marketing approaches as well as the changing landscape that caused this new role to be introduced across business. It sets up essential digital marketing concepts, including a basic understanding of tools, measurement concepts and an overview of best practices for brand, targeting, content strategy (a pillar of digital marketing) and engagement.

Chapter 2, 'The Role of the Digital Marketer', sets out to show the specific skills and approaches required as the digital marketer interacts with other business disciplines and with the external community of social influencers directly. Unlike traditional marketing, which afforded a greater distance between marketer and consumer, digital marketers must often work directly with the customers they look to influence. They must often be more technology-savvy and technology-driven than traditional marketers, and these role distinctions will be covered in depth.

What kinds of tools, methods and techniques should a digital marketer master and continue to improve upon? That nuts and bolts answer is detailed in **Chapter 3**, 'Tools, Methods and Techniques', which acts as a survey of the field at the time of publication as well as an evergreen analysis on how to handle the urgency associated with new types of tools and platforms. Within each business you serve, you will need to establish digital marketing processes and frameworks for handling content, creative agencies and integrations with other marketers in the firm. You will need to offer stakeholders frequent updates on how a campaign is going and coordinate across departments to achieve marketing goals. This chapter digs into the daily rhythm of digital marketing work, and while every employment situation will be different, it will likely require some or all of the practices mentioned in this chapter.

Chapter 4, 'Next Steps for the Digital Marketer', looks ahead to the career path that continued development of those skills identified in Chapters 2 and 3 offers. This chapter discusses role variations, from entry level to senior director, from specialisations like search engine marketing to broader entrepreneurial roles.

The 'A Day in the Life of a Digital Marketer' case study chapter, **Chapter 5**, includes a fictional narrative of how a digital marketing intern might interact with various mentors and colleagues inside a business. Carl's daily rounds and quizzing of various professionals are drawn from examples within the business experiences of the two authors, so while not a case study in the traditional academic sense, it is the easiest way to communicate in real terms the multi-faceted day-to-day reality of a digital marketer.

1 OVERVIEW OF THE DIGITAL MARKETING FIELD

This chapter introduces the broad category of digital marketing and positions this within the professional marketing field. It emphasises recent technological platforms as marketing channels and discusses how to take advantage of advances in marketing analytics. The chapter also includes the bridging of old and new marketing concepts.

These are fundamentals upon which the book will build its premise: exploring the digital marketer role and its many facets.

TRADITIONAL VS. DIGITAL MARKETING

Let's start this chapter by looking at traditional marketing vs. digital marketing.

Firstly, think about all the ways businesses have traditionally reached out to their customers (or potential customers) to create brand awareness or bring about a sale.

Take a look at the examples below, ranked in order from free to most expensive:

1. Word-of-mouth. A satisfied customer can often be the best advertising.
2. Favourable mention in a community bulletin, such as a church or school newsletter – possibly in relation to a charitable or joint project with those institutions.

3. An organic club or community of product users arises – think book club, motorcycle or car club and so on.

4. Favourable mention in a newspaper or on television or radio as the product is talked about in the news or the founder of the company is interviewed by the press.

5. Paid advertisement in a newspaper, radio ad or television.

6. Paid endorsement by a celebrity or person of status in a media channel.

7. Presence in a physical location – a stall at a community Sunday market, space in a consignment shop, all the way up to an ongoing storefront in an expensive location.

Now, think about how these translate to the digital realm – sometimes they are cheaper and sometimes they need more work (the physical realm has physical costs and limits on how many messages can come at a human being, but digital channels have no physical limits other than the user's attention span).

1. **Word-of-mouth.** A new customer can hear about your product or service from their friends through a digital channel they have already opted into – such as Facebook, Twitter, Instagram, Pinterest or Snapchat. Because this recommendation, like the in-person word-of-mouth counterpart, relies on social ties, it can be very effective as the speaker on your behalf already has the potential customer's trust.

2. **Favourable mention in a community publication.** In this case, recommendation of your product on an online forum where like-minded people gather (think car enthusiasts, followers of certain rock bands and so on) works a bit like word-of-mouth. Forum users are usually familiar with each other and self-selected as people of like mind on consumption of specific content or other topics. Trust is higher

than an interruptive advertisement because a recommendation is embedded in a topic that the users already care about.

3. **Community.** One of the best outcomes for a product is that an online community arises around your product or service itself. In this case, fans of your line of gadgetry, home repair techniques or other examples of your product will be discussing your product with each other. While this does create an obligation for you to deal with customer support issues and hear complaints about your product or service, this kind of community creates fertile ground for you to offer previews, exclusive content tutorials, discounts and announcements of new products or services members will want to buy right away.

4. **Earned media.** This kind of publicity can work against a company, as when a flaw in a product is discovered or some scandal with the business leaders arises, but it is marketing that the company does not have to pay for directly and digital marketers will be looking to maximise positive outcomes here.

5. **Paid media.** This includes marketing channels such as Twitter, Facebook and YouTube with the aim of raising awareness of a product, acquiring customers or converting people to a sale. Online channels could report engagement and if instrumented properly, conversion, with high precision. So, money must be spent here but it is possible to understand how successful or problematic that spend is ahead of time. Careful pilots and monitoring of analytics from the campaign assist with this.

6. **Celebrity endorsement.** To use this approach, the digital marketer will need cash, early assessment of whether the celebrity or influencer is the right fit for the target audience of your product and careful fine-tuning of the contract or relationship.

7. **Digital presence.** Here, ongoing digital presence translates to digital channels and locations where

3

your customers can be immersed in your brand and message, as well as order your products or services. This is where you make your digital stamp upon the world and well-informed consumers will look you up, for example, 'does this business have a website?', 'can I email someone at the business to set up an appointment?', 'can I book an appointment online?', 'can I purchase their product without leaving my house?' Such a presence may include shopping cart technology so people can pay for your product or service.

The digital marketer will need to take on the challenge of mixing and matching these techniques in a way that best supports their business. For example, some businesses may have customers that are not on broad social media platforms; some businesses may have customers in a demographic that heavily uses one digital channel and not another (think game walkthroughs on YouTube or Twitch) and some businesses may find their customers are in transition from traditional to digital means of communication.

The seismic marketing shift

The key changes between traditional and digital marketing over the past few years fall into these categories:

1. **Speed** from concept to execution. What might take months traditionally, for example, a magazine going to press, can take days digitally, for example, an online publication highlighting the marketing message.

2. **Democratisation** of taste making – where once it was the designers and fashion critics solely holding forth on what New York or London or Paris said were the trends, now Instagram, lifestyle Pinterest boards and fashion blogs command as much or more social cachet of taste making.

3. **Enhanced analytics** – with technology platforms able to give deeper analysis automatically of what

users are doing online, the digital marketer can now know their customers more accurately than they ever could in the analogue world.

4. **Higher emphasis on relationship and community-building** – while in other eras it might have taken years for word-of-mouth and geographic barriers to be overcome for a business, now the internet allows businesses to have paying customers at a far remove. Social discourse online now needs active management of brand or product perception on a 24 hours a day, seven days a week basis.

5. **Rapid change** in the customer landscape – what is signal today may become irrelevant noise tomorrow. Digital marketers must continually keep abreast of technology advances and public sentiment shifts as the online conversations continue.

Changes in basic approach and the marketer role

How has this seismic shift in marketing played out? Let's look first at the expectations and basic skills of the traditional marketer and then compare that with those expected of digital marketers.

Digital marketers, coming on the heels of traditional marketers, get to make use of techniques from both worlds (and should, since their target audiences may live in both spaces).

Traditional

In the past, traditional marketing skills encompassed such areas as creating a marketing plan with messaging, value propositions and key goals that could be broken down into separate strategic initiatives and then further into action plans. Once the marketer was focused on a promotional marketing initiative and broke that further into its components or action plans, they would need the skills to address the following tasks:

1. Testing the proposed message or branding on focus groups or simply ad hoc customer groups that

could be depended on to give critical and necessary feedback. Since this message drives the content, knowing that it resonates first is best before actually creating the meat of the campaign.

2. Strategising and executing on creative collateral, including:

   a. Copywriting for magazine and newspaper advertisements.

   b. Working with media professionals to create radio or TV broadcast ads.

   c. Making use of designers and layout professionals to create stunning brochures or other such conference booth materials.

   d. Understanding effective pitch language for direct mail advertisements and the demographics of paid mailing lists.

3. Working by oneself or with a team, executing the actual delivery of the creative materials to the specifications of the advertising industry, conference or in-person presentation requirements or getting collateral to mailing distributors.

4. A traditional marketer, while not an accountant, still has to account for every expenditure and understand the finances within a marketing strategy, such as:

   a. Controlling and accounting for campaign costs: how much a coupon or in-store discount could be before it started cutting into the business, how much it costs to obtain a new customer, whether a campaign approach is effective, how much a buy-one-get-one-free offer encourages repeat business and so on.

   b. Understanding the limitations of a company's budget and the importance of this campaign within the company's goals. For example, as a start-up or a sole proprietorship gets going, less is known about what will be effective for it and its customers. The company may need more marketing in the first year compared to one year later, and it may need to spend more to set the baseline for further optimisation.

c. Understanding any seasonality that affected the ability to promote. So, for example, you would not try to make waves in the news for your product launch if you knew that the nation's focus would be on that week's football match, and it would be hard to get them to pay attention to other, non-football related concerns.

Digital marketing

Digital marketing still needs a lot of the same thinking as traditional marketing, but technological advances make a lot of things easier to research and deliver. Digital marketing also builds more upon relationships – as interactions in the digital world can be easier to track, it becomes easier to understand what your customers respond to.

For example, to test a brand message or product idea, a business could get feedback on social media – through a Facebook page or Twitter account, asking for information from customers and the public for free. While not as scientific as a research study, for someone like a hairstylist or shop proprietor, finding out when most of their customers would like them to be available (Saturday evenings or Sunday evenings, for example) delivers real benefit. Supportive and engaged customers, once you win their trust, are often the best advocates for your business and can help you to understand how to make more money from them if you create and nurture the proper relationship.

If you are trying to design appealing logos or graphics to distinguish a business, there are online marketplaces of design freelancers where you can peruse their offerings while still working conceptually to nail down your own approach. You can surf the web, finding competitors and studying their online approach to content and presentation, and search for marketing appearances. YouTube is an endless source of videos by both personal and business creators, some using only their phones or cheap podcasting equipment to make compelling viral videos.

And finally, because the digital attention span of humans does have limits, a digital marketer will be able to make use of digital marketing analytics tools to understand the effectiveness of a campaign, often in real time. Most search engine and social media platforms that take paid advertising have dashboards that explain how effective a reach your marketing had, how the ads were targeted and how long it took until the spend limit was reached.

OUTBOUND AND INBOUND MARKETING

Marketing can be outbound or inbound; let's look at this.

Outbound marketing

Outbound marketing, especially if you are new to the field of marketing, is what you think of most as a consumer. A company or person reaches out to you in several ways to get you to buy their goods or service through advertising, phone calls, door-to-door flyers, direct postal mailings and so on. As the consumer, this kind of marketing may seem interruptive or a side-product of a consumer society with leisure time. The business places their brand or advertisement in the consumer's context, where they think their customers are, and without the customers expecting to see their message; for example, surprise takeover or creation of a small art gallery in London to sell your goods or promote your service, or a billboard placed on a road in Montana in the United States.

Roughly speaking, the process is:

1. Create a campaign that appeals to as broad an audience as you can (to increase the chances of hitting your customer).
2. Time the campaign to capture attention in a certain venue, place or context (ads on the subway, flyer in the home letterbox).
3. Determine from the volume of sales or service bookings during and after the campaign whether it worked.

4. Start up a new campaign again as you decide you need more customers.

Inbound marketing

Inbound marketing, by contrast, is a term coined by HubSpot chief executive officer (CEO) Brian Halligan, but identical in principle to the ideas put forth by Seth Godin in his book *Permission Marketing* (1999).[1] Godin felt that the most effective methods of marketing got the customers' buy-in or consent. Other US marketers, including HubSpot, have promoted the 'get found' approach. In the digital realm, a digital marketer creates and provides content for a company blog, podcast, ebook or email list that the interested customer can sign up for. With such an approach, the business is making it worthwhile for the customer to find and engage them.

To attract customers, you offer something of value (usually content) for free, closely aligned with your brand, and you keep doing it continually: a blog, an online seminar, engagement in social media, live chats on Twitter. You are wooing them rather than trying to do a hard sell at once.

Once you have attracted the right kind of customer, you must convert them to align with your brand. Ideally this is the exchange of promised value from the attraction phase – you send them a free ebook on home repair for example, to get their email address for your marketing list. Or they watch your free podcast to understand how to do something that is in their own interest and, in the process, see how your product helps them achieve their goals.

The 'close' is the opportunity to market to the customer again and repeat the sale or repeat the wooing to make them even more delighted with your company or brand. Marketing to customers who have bought something becomes easier because now you have a relationship and, if pleased with your product, they will want to know the next time it goes on sale, gets an upgrade or an updated version is produced.

Inbound marketing is ongoing and analytical. Instead of the traditional beginning and end of a campaign, the marketing becomes part of the company's lifestyle and infrastructure. The digital marketer is the one who helps the company at all stages of this inbound marketing process, including analysing if and how much the strategies are working.

MEASURING AND ANALYSING

Whether the digital marketer serves themselves as a business owner, helps a charitable organisation or is part of a corporate digital team that works on behalf of a large organisational division, they will need to consider carefully how they measure their success and how they will study the landscape to ensure proper targeting and uptake of their content.

Considering the measurement needs and tools of measurement at the beginning of the process of creating a digital campaign helps to keep the campaign itself oriented to the right goals, and ensures that if something goes wrong or a course correction is needed there are signals and opportunity to do so.

Because of the opportunity for real-time measurement on many social media platforms and advertising platforms, digital spend can also be one of the most effective uses of money – given that the digital marketer is able to course-correct a failing campaign right as it is detected. Real-time measurement can also show differences between platforms in their performance, and the digital marketer can adjust accordingly.

In Figure 1.1 there are some basic concepts of traditional marketing success measurement, adapted to the digital age. As technology changes, the precise terms for each platform may vary but the marketing concepts and principles will be constant.

Figure 1.1 The marketing funnel

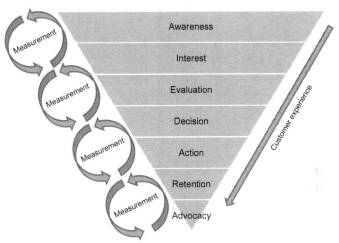

REACH AND ENGAGEMENT

Reach is essentially what the audience for your marketing content is on a perfect day. It describes the best upper bounds of your campaign. Obviously, the extent to which people are exposed to your campaign will depend on multiple factors – the marketing channels or platforms that you used to deliver the message, consumer preference or interest that day and how well executed the content and campaign itself was in reaching its ideal recipients.

Organic reach is the amount of exposure your campaign would field without spending any money – the people who already follow your blog and read it daily, the number of normal visitors to your website, the number of people who do a search and find that your business is ranked at the top through sheer relevance. Often, marketers need to enhance their reach to target new customers and encourage their loyalty, so organic measures will not go far enough.

Reach is described in multiple ways depending on the nature of the campaign. Reach can be earned or viral (a social media personality praises your company without thought of payment for example, or a video created by a fan goes madly viral on YouTube) or paid (if so, the advertising platform has multiple ways to ensure that you get the reach you paid for and that it is targeted properly).

Reach must be evaluated in terms of your goal (see the marketing funnel in Figure 1.1). If all you want is awareness, the higher the number of people who are exposed to your message and your brand the more successful you are. If your aim is to have them sign up to be emailed your newsletter, get them to call the salesperson or buy your product online, then sheer numbers of random people will not work. Targeted outreach, exposing only those you really are likely to get as customers, is more efficient and will save the digital marketer time and money. Remember, everything in addition to organic reach costs your company something out of the marketing budget – so additional mechanisms to amplify your reach for free (viral spreading of your videos on YouTube, word-of-mouth) help. Also, careful examination of the advertising platform metrics, demographics and approach before signing on to expand the campaign's reach in a certain direction is wise. As a digital marketer, the company will be relying on your analytical skills as well as intuitive understanding of the customer to make sure the reach you pay for is the right reach.

Engagement is the next goal, after attaining proper reach to your campaign. The customer has seen the message: how did they react to it? Ideally, they took the action you requested in the call to action part of your message or their perception of your brand shifted for the better. Answering back on social media, signing up to follow your social media accounts and making a purchase are all good signs of engagement for the digital marketer. At the end of the day, reaching potential customers will not be enough – the digital marketer looks for the customer to reach back.

GOOD PRACTICES

Digital marketing, dependent as it is on ever-changing technology platforms and the tastes of a changing population, is a field that will see best practices continue to evolve. Where in an earlier decade, digital outreach might have been innovative if it used video or Facebook giveaways, for certain markets they may seem de rigueur or even too commonplace to be worthwhile. Like all marketing, digital marketing must work to outpace fad and fancy, and instead work diligently to predict and manage outcomes. Still, organising principles and best practices still exist within digital marketing and can be used whatever the campaign, whatever the season.

Brand

Whilst a brand, especially an older one, may have been established outside the digital realm, it is imperative that digital marketing efforts are consistent with the personal brand of the proprietor or aligned with the corporate brand of the business. A brand is not a static concept: actions taken on behalf of the brand alter the brand, just as the brand's influence and expectation-setting among customers highly influences how they will hear the digital messages. Digital marketing is most effective when it supports intrinsic brand continuity and authenticity, even if the work it is doing is to shift customers' perception. Without a coherent framework to tell the story, digital marketing can fail. Part of that framework is the branding established by the firm.

Digital marketers should always work to:

1. **Focus their brand.** For consultants, shop proprietors or others who make their living by being their brand, admonitions around presenting a focused and authentic presence are even more firm. Just as you would find it hard to have a conversation with someone who seemed scattered, moody, unpredictable and sometimes not even the same personality type, so do customers have difficulty in parsing a scattered brand.

2. **Determine brand boundaries.** Yes, as a human being the business owner is complex and as a consultant may have several specialties and skills to offer. Yes, the personal brand for that individual needs to be selling all those skills. But the customers interacting with that individual need to feel they are talking to a person, with a clear professional personality, and a tone they can count on to be reasonable. For example, the tone of certain tell-all social media personalities or lifestyle consultants may be beyond the pale of what a dentist or shop owner would want to project but for them, because their business relies upon this full-frontal candour and their community follows them for those disclosures, it results in more web traffic or consultations.

3. **Incorporate friendly helpfulness.** Often the most effective branding strategy for the business or the sole proprietor is to incorporate helpfulness into the brand. A social stream of constantly useful tips, related to the central business, entices people to follow whether they use the product or not. Conversation with customers about what they want to see or how they are using the product and offering customer support when things go awry are all extensions of the helpfulness you can include in your branding and marketing strategies.

Targeting

Some of the best practices around respectful and accurate targeting for your digital marketing campaigns are legal ones. If you need to ask for a customer to opt in to your message, subscribe or unsubscribe, review personal data that will be used in the marketing campaign or give approvals for release (as for photo and video likenesses), always do so. It is up to the digital marketer to research the laws around permission and customer data.

Digital marketing, being based on principles of permission and engagement, is most effective when the campaign is compelling to the audience and aimed at the right audience. A customer will find an ad for an irrelevant product (golf clubs when they are a tennis player for example) more annoying and intrusive than a customer whose tastes are matched by the ads they see. The digital marketer knows that the public has a limited number of hours in the day and a limited amount of focused attention it can give to any message at any given moment.

Sometimes, this is best demonstrated in the timing, frequency and context of the digital message being shown.

Targeting as a mechanism for customer delight can backfire. Facebook is an expert in targeted advertising (since it encourages its users to create comprehensive profiles with attributes that its advertisers can utilise across their campaigns) but it's memory posting reminders (such as 'a year ago you became friends on Facebook with this person') appeared tone deaf to customers who had lost a relationship or a loved one or pet, and did not want to be reminded of that loss. As another example, customers complain about content on websites where they get a popup ad or display banner with each change of web page – news outlets and general interest sites showing a selection of images in a gallery format often include different ads with each loaded image, which slows down page load times and frustrates users, especially those with low bandwidth speeds.

Improper context might be the most damaging to the brand of all. For example, Google had to start a new programme with its largest advertisers on YouTube to help them ensure their advertising would not appear on videos incompatible with their brand values, as opposed to letting their ads run on any YouTube video. Activists and community leaders are watching and the appearance of popular US brands advertising on the controversial US political site Breitbart, as another example (even though it was done through an ad network the brands had no control over), drove them to pressure many companies to remove advertising from that site.

Content

At the centre of all digital campaigns is the content, the actual messaging or digital offering that the marketers present to potential customers. Like the technology of digital media channels and social media, kinds of digital content will expand over the years to come. The surface areas and media types that will arise for the digital marketer to utilise will grow exponentially as our technology-driven lifestyle does.

Self-driving cars, cooperative driving pool car services and shifting modes of public transport may carve out new areas for digital marketers to explore. Augmented reality (AR) headsets and interactive stores may replace the simpler QR codes and interactive graphics in place today. Future customers may be wearing chips inside their hands instead of battery-powered wearables. Robots may serve us and carry out advertising of the future while they do their duties. Still, the digital marketer will have to follow key practices for content regardless of the format, media type, channel or platform.

1. **Make it engaging.** Digital content should be concise, clear and catchy. Whether it is a 280-character tweet, a video clip, a marketing jingle or an advertisement by a robot, the piece of content should be no longer than it needs to be. It should clearly convey the value proposition of the product or at least the tone the product wishes to be associated with. And hardest of all, it must be catchy, memorable, delightful – worth the cost of the attention the customer has given to the content.

2. **Viral and shareable.** It must be the kind of content that people are glad to be associated with. Creating this content quality is the challenge of the digital marketer and their allies, but it also pertains to the form factor. If the average person's mobile phone will not support downloading or sharing a long video, then the digital marketer must make it possible to share the link to said video. If the message can be conveyed in an animated gif instead of a video,

and that gif is small enough to work for people of limited bandwidth, the message becomes even more effective.

Twitter has long been an interesting medium for marketers – not necessarily always for their campaign demographics but because the virality of Twitter is contained in a small space. The platform itself has had to do work around photos and video and support of animated gifs to expand advertising capabilities. But a digital marketer would do well to study short-form mediums like Twitter or Tumblr because of the message compression and economical use of language involved with using them as a marketing platform.

Engagement

To create a great relationship with your customers, you need to think about the best ways to approach each campaign to handle customer engagement. The six Cs that circle your relationship and community engagement strategy are presented below. They should be easy to control.

1. **Creation:** Create specific places for problem solving, away from other forms of marketing.

   Just as the content needs to be worth spreading to others, the digital marketer must plan for the kinds of relationship the business should have with its customers. Social media channels are a very public way for a company to be called to task for not offering customer support. If the brand or company does not want to be talking about private matters in public, they must plan and create channels for escalation of technical problems and refunds, preferably away from potential customers.

2. **Collaboration:** Create the right infrastructure and staffing.

   Here, the digital marketer must work efficiently with the staff on hand such that there are processes and templates to expedite customer satisfaction.

A set email address, a web contact form, a voicemail system that only goes to the start-up customer support person's inbox are all examples of the collaboration and infrastructure that may be needed to underpin a successful discount campaign or marketing giveaway.

3. **Communication:** Structure your content for high levels of responsiveness.

   Strategies must be employed so that a company can continue to scale responses to a campaign or piece of content while doing necessary business tasks, especially if the digital marketer is the only member of marketing staff. Using platforms that allow for scheduled posts, tweets or other forms of publishing can be helpful, as can mobile apps that allow a business owner to check the success of a campaign while in transit.

   Study your customers' patterns – do they peruse your site on weekends more than weekdays? Careful planning also helps: is Tuesday a holiday or special buying event for your product and you will need extra help managing the incoming social media or orders, for example?

4. **Consistency:** Pace yourself and be consistent in your approach whenever possible.

   Until your company has the funds to hire more people, it may well be you handling an ever-increasing customer base, so choose methods of work that allow you to scale your customer service and lessen context switching. You may set aside 9 to 10 a.m. as your hour each day for focused answering of customer emails and tweets. You are then able to work on the business until 4 to 5 p.m. when you close out the day having handled other issues that arise. You could configure your phone to alert you when customers are posting or tweeting at your account, and you can maximise your commute by using your phone app to respond while making other appointments.

Having said that about consistency, note that: (a) a new business may not yet have set patterns; and (b) to get a reputation for flawless customer service you often need to be alert and responsive as much of the time as your customers are online, trying to engage with you. In the beginning, you can expect an extensive ramp up while you respond throughout the day, and only later be able to see patterns that enable you to optimise.

5. **Customer focus:** Set boundaries and respond to customers at your best.

    The other aspect of this fast-paced lifestyle is that you will eventually be working too quickly, be physically sick or tired when you should be responding to a customer. Ideally, you or your team would have already set protocols about what to do in an emergency or bad public relations (PR) situation and rules about tone and decision making around controversial or difficult PR responses. If there is an apology to be made in public, on digital media, it is better to have decided the course of action, and who is the spokesperson, well in advance of the actual crisis.

    At your best here means not only buttoned-up, thorough, thoughtful and with the best service of your customer in mind – it also means authentic. Just as you would not appear on your neighbour's doorstep unkempt and undressed, you would also not want to hesitate in apologising for how your chickens tore up their garden either. A good neighbour would make amends; so too would a good corporate citizen. What you can say and do may be limited by your legal department or company policy, so it is always wise to check, but time after time brands get in trouble for being too arrogant. Thoughtful, ethical, authentic and personable are the better notes to hit.

6.   **Creativity:** Find ways of integrating digital with your other marketing campaigns.

This integration may be as simple as putting a sign up in your shop about a 20 per cent off sale and posting on a social media channel that the sale is on for today only. It may be as complicated as buying TV ads, search engine ads, email blasts on various community sites and coordinating five guest video blogs and podcasts to centre around the same week. Again, the idea is that the digital marketing amplifies and expands the reach and reinforcement of the message and encourages customer engagement.

Marketing campaigns that rely on different channels often require project management to plan which of the channels most time should be spent on (to buy space for an online ad or message, to create complicated media assets, to obtain the proper time slot, to find or set up the proper relationships and so on). Television ads and TV or movie product placements may take the longest to bear fruit. Television advertising must be produced, slotted and paid for ahead of time through the proper industry channels. As movies can be made years ahead, product placement in a movie needs to be done while the movie (or television show) is in development.

On the speedier side, you can place last-minute search engine advertising or upload your ad for a Facebook campaign in a matter of minutes. Here, however, you must strategise wisely both in your budget and in your targeting.

Google and Facebook make use of auction technology – both companies are pioneering work in their respective spaces – so that often your message placement costs are approximated. If more people want the same demographic audience or keywords you choose, then you will pay more.

Again, each channel that is integrated into your campaign must be part of the overall execution approach for your message. Ideally, your content in one channel reinforces content in another channel, so that the message sticks in the users' minds without becoming annoying, leading them to that all-important engagement. Different channels have different audience overlap capabilities and these must be carefully considered. Is your goal brand loyalty or new customers or both? Is your target the folks that crossover between two mediums often?

Documentation

Integrated marketing campaigns need various levels of documentation, such as:

- a vision document, storyboard, mood board, taste chart;
- value proposition and message effectiveness testing documents;
- integrated marketing calendar.

A vision document varies by company but it should detail the company's overall requirements for the product to be marketed in the campaign. It should showcase the overall product in general terms including its mission and value and may incorporate such components as a storyboard, mood board or taste chart to flesh out more of the concepts and guidelines.

The storyboard can be something as simple as a set of sticky notes about the customer issues and how the brand can solve them. It could be complex, with documentation, graphics or videos at every stage of the customer story. Fortunately, each part of the story is an opportunity for the digital marketer to use topics such as blog posts, social posts or visuals for customers. Each step is an opportunity to educate or inform the customer, whilst the marketing team move on to the next step in the journey.

A mood board or taste chart is a way of getting at the emotional value or flavour of a campaign. It is often a collage of words and visual images used to convey the feeling the marketing campaign or brand is supposed to convey. Just as many car commercials show the driver on winding roads in lush mountainside terrain, mood boards get at the feeling you want people to have for your product and not just the details of how a campaign might be waged.

SUMMARY

In this chapter we have examined traditional marketing and digital marketing concepts, foundational metrics for evaluating success and key approaches to branding, content, targeting and engagement that are the cornerstones of the digital marketing practice. Throughout the book, we will refer back to these concepts in order to discuss the day-to-day activities of the digital marketer role and the skills that must be continually honed to best serve business needs.

2 THE ROLE OF THE DIGITAL MARKETER

This chapter explains more about how you, as the digital marketer, can help your business, and covers what the role does uniquely to achieve brand recognition, consistent messaging, customer engagement and sales.

Also included in the chapter is an examination of the kinds of skills a digital marketer needs to use while intersecting with other business disciplines and how to work with traditional marketers within your company to achieve better results. Technology and soft skills go hand in hand to achieve success in this role.

A GREAT CAREER CHOICE

Digital marketing is a constantly evolving industry. As more companies evolve their marketing efforts to embrace online media, roles evolve to fit the new marketing methods. It helps level the online playing field; it shapes the future of the marketing landscape. A small company can have the resources to deliver sales and marketing processes that were previously only available to large organisations – even without the extra budget or resources.

Digital communications are more versatile, efficient, interactive, cost-effective and measurable.

Customers spend a lot of time online and their online behaviour can be tracked and monitored. They can be influenced by what they see online; their purchasing behaviour can be changed to suit the marketer's campaign. Internet marketing tools can be used to interact and engage with customers in real time.

It makes sense for marketers to embrace this new form of communication. They can increase their digital reach, improve brand awareness and strengthen their existing relationships with their customers. They can engage with them through social media and steal the march on their competitors, learning how to improve their own campaigns as they watch how others perform. All this is digital marketing – the domain of the digital marketer.

A digital marketer must be a doer and a translator. He or she discerns digital marketing opportunities for the business, enables the business to take advantage of them, while also ensuring these efforts integrate with any greater marketing efforts across the company.

Becoming a digital marketer is a great career choice. There are a lot of strands to consider: from search engine optimisation (SEO) to copywriting, analytics to advertising, email marketing to social media marketing.

Digital media is fast overtaking traditional media. As this rapidly changing market develops through technology, your role as a digital marketer will also need to adapt to keep up with newly released technologies. Marketers can focus on one sector of marketing, switch to other sectors, or move from corporate to agency marketing as their career evolves and grows.

Digital marketers can often progress to becoming marketing executives or transfer to other parts of the business, based on the insights and technical knowledge they accumulate during their careers. Or, they can step off the corporate track entirely and found their own companies – with solid knowledge of how to use the tools of the digital age to promote their products and services.

According to a survey by Smart Insights,[1] over half of organisations do digital activities without a digital marketing strategy. Only one-third have a digital marketing strategy that is integrated with their marketing strategies. Clearly there is more work to be done and a clear need for digital marketers to do it.

It is a rollercoaster of a ride, trying to keep up – but one thing is for sure: with a career as a digital marketer, you will never be bored with your job.

The future of digital marketing

Almost half of the world uses the internet with 46.1 per cent of the world's population logging on in 2016 according to internet live stats on the web.[2] That means that 3.42 billion of the 7.43 billion people across the world have access to the internet: a massive marketing opportunity for digital marketers around the globe.

A small amount of cash currently enables you, the digital marketer, to create an online campaign that has the potential to reach a huge amount of people. Campaign results are easy to measure, customer perception and satisfaction happens in real time and brand reputations can be made – or ruined – in just a few mouse clicks.

The Internet of Things (IoT) does (to some extent) and will continue to provide a terrific opportunity for digital marketers. The IoT is a potentially unlimited network of items fitted with sensors and transmitters that can communicate with each other and pass reports back to a central management console.

Fitness wearables, automobiles, even credit cards, dog tags and travel passes can communicate with host systems and provide permission-based in-depth analysis and consumer behaviour data.

Brands can collect data on exactly where their products are being used and via the IoT will soon be able to notify companies when a product such as running shoes needs to be replaced.[3]

Health companies could also get access to this real-time data, offering fitness tips, advice and supplements to the person who wants to get fit, stay healthy, lose weight and so on.

Technology is always evolving. Whether it is the development of a new app, a wearable, cloud-based voice service or automated robot, digital marketing is at the forefront of these trends.

DIGITAL MARKETER SKILLS

The previous chapter briefly covered the various kinds of tasks a digital marketer is called upon to do. All those tasks will be impacted by the level of strategic skill brought to bear in three major areas – PR, traditional marketing and channel or platform expertise.

If you come from a traditional background, here is where you can see your acumen bear fruit and provide a foundation for integrated traditional and digital campaigns.

Public relations skills

Whether new to marketing or a traditional marketer making the transition to digital, the digital marketer still needs to rely on the strengths seen in those coming from a traditional PR and marketing background.

Marketing and promotional skills

Public relations skills, such as writing an announcement in such a way that the press or news outlets are interested, matters even more in an era where journalists are finding and developing sources and stories from posts on social media.

You need an understanding of the news cycle in your community – for example, are feel good stories written for the weekends, with hard-hitting business news appearing first thing Monday morning? This will help with timing posts, tweets or photojournalism where it can catch the eye of a reporter.

PR professionals also develop an uncanny understanding of when **not** to call attention to their company or product. Perhaps there is a national controversy and they do not want the brand associated with either side. Perhaps a competitor is experiencing a PR disaster – do they jump in and skewer their opponent or do they take the high road? Knowing when to avoid 'breaking in to jail' by being part of the conversation becomes doubly important, as the digital marketer has many opportunities for meaningful conversation and spotting which ones to join requires skill.

Bridging

Another important public relations skill that translates over to digital marketing is that of 'bridging'. In media interviews, this is getting the conversation shifted from what the reporter just asked back to the messaging or more comfortable spot for the company or brand to talk about. Done well it does not seem like deflecting a question, because the safer or promotional topic is neatly tied to the initial question. In social media, where the conversations with the public and one's customers may be prolonged, it is important to be able to shift them in this way. Acknowledge what the original question and intent was but also make sure to get your own company's message out there. In the war of perception, storytelling and careful language can make all the difference to your brand.

Presenting

Traditional PR involves public speaking and the digital marketer can make great use of these skills. Whether it is giving a speech that will be live-cast to conference attendees or creating a podcast in the home office, being able to communicate clearly and in a lively manner will aid in a digital marketing career. For sole proprietors who must self-market and handle their own sales, the ability to convey in person why a customer should buy your product or service is priceless. Some podcasters in digital media do so well they are paid to give talks to business audiences, and the marketer who has experience in public speaking will find their podcasting or social audience increases after a conference talk.

Traditional marketing skills

While parallels to traditional marketing will be drawn throughout this book, there are a few key mappings that digital marketers will find useful.

Broad marketing understanding and ability to integrate

As mentioned previously, the new world of digital marketing is one of integration. It is not enough to rely on traditional marketing measures to get the word out; your audience gives their attention to digital platforms daily and so any real-world outcome (a weekend sale at your shop, for example) must be supported in the virtual world as well.

These skills around integrating different components into a united marketing framework are carried down throughout each level of implementation. The digital marketer must ensure that their digital marketing plan is plugged into the whole of their business efforts. If you tweet a call to action, you must include a link to a web page, a phone number or email address that allows your customer to take real-world action. Ideally, the branding and messaging – even the form of the content – aligns with what the customer sees when they come to your place of business.

Integration skill also maps to people as well. If you are part of a team of digital marketers, you must share information and coordinate when your efforts take place for the greatest effect. You must be able to adapt your digital marketing plans to fit those of the traditional marketers for your business and be able to recommend what does and does not translate to the online space.

Adaption and re-use

Digital marketers, like traditional marketers, must have a keen sense of time and timing and the ability to adapt marketing messages to different mediums.

Online media works both as broadcast and asynchronous events. A tweet stream is available for everyone to peruse later, just as a chat transcript or transcribed television interview posted online would be. There is undeniable energy when people find themselves part of a group experience – live-tweeting an event or webcasting from a conference location or teaching an interactive online class. The digital marketer must be careful that the expressions that mean so much in that moment carry through to being read or perused at a later stage. If they do not, supplementing after the fact with video clips, blog posts or other explanations to create the context of the now-ended digital event helps. For example, Storify is a tool that digital marketers can use to turn tweetstorms into unified stories or blog posts that capture the sequence and the reactions to the event.

Some firms put television advertisements on YouTube channels or other locations to further their reach. But this sharing sensibility can also backfire, as online consumers mash-up and re-mix your video into other contexts. Companies themselves may opt to re-mix video content specifically for online purposes or hold a contest for their customers where the best remix or new creation advertising the product wins a prize. Just as internet memes seem to take the collective mindset of the public by storm, so too could your digital marketing message.

Internet memes are typically amusing quotes or blocks of text added to an image or video, designed to propagate and be shared across social media sites in a viral way. Images of Grumpy Cat with associated text blocks are good examples of internet memes.

Audience targeting and segmentation

Audience targeting and segmentation in traditional marketing is just as important to digital marketing, but technology platforms give it a new twist. Some venues, like Facebook, allow for extremely specific demographics and psychographics to be selected for ad campaigns. Other community of interest sites, because their online content appeals to niche audiences, can offer the digital marketer the same audience targeting as if they had to buy a direct postal mail list or research the neighbourhoods of London to make sure the message fell on the right ears. Experience in understanding cost per acquisition for new customers in traditional marketing approaches will help the seasoned marketer map their old skills to the new digital ones.

Creativity – Solo or in collaboration

Creativity matters whether one is a traditional marketer or a digital marketer. The snappy response to an ongoing tweetstorm, the new way of approaching the customer to charm them, the eye for experimental tactics and synthesising new campaigns – these are all important shared skills for traditional and digital marketers. Even if you as the marketer are not creating the posters, clip art, animated gif memes or videos you will be working with creative people to do so and must be able to think like one yourself.

Visual content

Both traditional and digital marketers rely on engaging visual content in their campaigns.

Teaching a digital marketer how to create multimedia content is well beyond the scope of this book. However, there is an inventory of skillsets which, whether the marketer does the work themselves or hires a creative agency to do it, will stand them in good stead as they compose and test their campaigns.

- **Photography and illustration:** Besides shooting photos or creating illustrations, the ability to process image files and combine different visual elements from these sources can be an integral part of your digital campaign. Sole proprietors or consultants who need to establish their personal brand would do well to have professional-quality photographs taken, to include them on professional networking sites such as linkedin.com, as well as the social media platforms where they are establishing a presence. Likewise, a professional-quality logo for one's business is key (and will be a repeated element) to many kinds of digital campaigns.

- **Animation:** Fortunately, animated gif creator tools are abundant on the web, and one can do professional-level quality with Adobe's suite of tools for making Flash animations. For viral commentary or engaging with influencers, sometimes it does not pay to have the response look too slick. Video clips with text may be all that you need to get a meme across.

- **Data visualisation or design:** Being able to display a lot of data in an easy-to-digest format will stand the digital marketer in good stead for much of their career. In addition to internal reports, where one must explain the results of one's campaigns, being able to present data clearly and simply can help in external marketing as well. Not every case for your business can be summed up in non-verbal aesthetic though; sometimes the business-to-business (B2B) case needs to be proved with numbers.

Crafting a powerful video often means the shorter, the better. Facebook and Nielsen research[4] found that up to 47 per cent of the value in a video campaign was delivered in the first three seconds, while up to 74 per cent of the value was delivered in the first 10 seconds. Many users will be viewing your video on their phones as they wait to do something else. And their setup may not be particularly video ad friendly, so video creators must be careful to design for users who have auto-play, or their volume muted (e.g., if they are at work).

- **Video:** Entire books and online tutorials have been written on creating beautiful videos, with their attendant skillsets of camerawork, staging, lighting, sound, subtitles and more. A digital marketer would do well to hire an agency if the video output is expected to be complex or like a broadcast, such as a TV ad in video format. For the shoestring marketer, the camera may be an iPhone taped into position or a web camera. Stuck there overnight in 2014, Canadian Richard Dunn filmed a tribute video in the Las Vegas airport, lip syncing to Celine Dion's 'All by myself'.[5] Celine Dion invited Dunn and his family to one of her concerts and he got a book deal out of the experience.

Copyright/Rights Management

Digital marketers do not have to be lawyers, but they do have to research and understand what they can and cannot do when creating online content. Using photographs, excerpting clips from movies, TV shows or other videos on YouTube carry certain risks, particularly if the use is commercial and not personal or academic. Likewise, the amazing soundtrack to your launch video will have to be researched for licensing and the right to use the song with your brand.

- **Virtual reality (VR):** Major software companies such as Apple, Facebook, Google and Microsoft have released VR hardware and software packages. VR and AR will enable marketers to connect with their customers in a more immersive way. Customers can be immersed in a demonstration so that they can make a more informed choice about the product. VR can demonstrate the brand mission, generate buzz and excitement, and visually show how the brand can fit into the customer's aspirations. There is a vast, untapped market for VR and AR applications.

Goldman Sachs has predicted that the industry will reach a value of $80 billion by 2025.[6] Although AR does not mean that marketers create a whole new reality, they can enhance what already exists. If this is done successfully, the customer's experience will be improved providing that the applications can be tightly integrated into the existing customer journey.

Audio content

As audiences lean toward more multimedia experiences or download material to be heard during a gym workout or while commuting to work and so on, the digital marketer must consider the importance of sound and music to their marketing content. Likewise, the digital marketer may be required to master skills specific to audio to get their work done, such as the following:

- **Sound engineering or recording (for podcasting):** Skills here involve understanding the limitations and capabilities of microphones, how to clean up a file of its background noise to focus on the podcast and mixing in other sounds or music. As this is also an entire discipline unto itself, the digital marketer can choose how deep to become involved in this area. Certainly, someone can record off their laptop or phone and edit with various free tools available for this purpose. A handy resource by Atlantic Public Media, intended to train journalists interested in public radio, is: http://transom.org/tag/podcast-basics/.

A trend to watch is voice-activated devices, like Amazon's Alexa, or personal mobile assistants like Apple's Siri, Google Now's voice commands and Microsoft's Cortana. As consumers move from shopping with keyboards to headphones or microphones, digital marketers will need to keep abreast of these trends, composing 'voiceover ads' to gain consumer attention.

33

- **Voice acting, narration and vlogging ('vlogs' for short):** In some instances, the digital marketer is not the technical whizz setting up the podcasting studio and hosting setup, but instead the talent in front of the microphone. Careful pronunciation for listeners and lively, articulate commentary are two skills that digital marketers will need to hone if they are to be the online voice of their brand or company.

Strategic thinking

Strategic thinking is a skill that maps well from the traditional marketing realm to the digital one. Though traditional marketing channels tend to be more predictable in cost and seasonality, they offer opportunities to change the direction of the industry and appeal to the public. In the digital marketing profession, due to the fleeting timespan in which to act on public sentiment, and the need for integrated campaigns, a keen sense of strategy is even more necessary. Keeping the overall goal of your company in mind – whether to get new customers, get more out of existing customers or establish your brand – is key when conditions around you are changing and you have a limited window in which to influence the social media conversation. It can be tempting to go for a short-term win and lose the overall goal.

Tactical execution

Once you have your strategy, then you will need to consider execution. Planning and attention to detail is another area of traditional marketing activities that translate well to digital activities. Just as you need a comprehensive and well-thought out marketing plan in traditional marketing, you also need to make careful plans for digital campaigns which may have as much or more moving parts because the digital channels are augmenting traditional ones. It cannot be stressed enough that the marketing plan must incorporate definitions of success and success metrics to accompany them, with key indicators that will serve as signals during the campaign as to how the campaign is faring. While the analytics programs may differ from traditional to digital, the need for monitoring and the ability to pull the plug on something that is not working remains.

Managing marketing projects

A key element of execution for any marketer is project management. From the lowest ranking marketer to marketing directors, the ability to drive a project or an initiative forward is key to success. As with planning, the details matter here – timelines, deadlines, windows of opportunity, asset availability, budget costs and avoiding overruns – and the details are where a traditional marketer *or* a digital marketer may find themselves struggling. Better to have laid out how the project should go, assessing time, resource, quality, risks and objectives, and then change that plan, than have no project plan and find oneself drifting further away from target and running over budget.

Familiarity with marketing metrics

Data analysis and market research have long been important to traditional marketers, but not every traditional marketer had to have these skills. In the digital marketing profession, online tools and companies that specialise in the behaviour of internet users mean every digital marketer will have at least glancing experience with a spreadsheet and generating visual charts to explain the numbers. Where social media platforms can offer you information on people's searching, or social media habits, you will end up doing market research even beyond the tried and true traditional marketing focus group and telephone surveys, simply because the tools enable you to see, at least in rudimentary terms, how your campaign is doing.

This additional insight can save the business money. A Twitter conversation between your brand and six avid customers may even alleviate the need to hold a focus group on your just-released product. Proficiency with Microsoft Excel, SQL and Google Analytics, or other web analytics programs tuned to the company website, will assist in either marketing role but is especially important to the digital marketer.

Business domain expertise

The main skills that carry over from traditional to digital marketing revolve around the marketer's understanding of their business and customer set. For example, a hat shop proprietor knows that a national holiday will see a rush of orders coming in at the last minute, and they would time their traditional marketing and digital campaigns right at the time customers would be planning attire for that day's events. Or, another firm knows that they get significant customer returns and customer support requests right after Boxing Day, so they amp up their social media coverage to field off negativity and to help concerned customers who may have bought the wrong item.

Customer focus or mindset

The other example of carry-over understanding lies in the mindset of the customers for the business. If the customers are not often on social media, but their children are, campaigns may be designed to have the younger set influence the older one. 'Look, Mum, a discount on digital cameras and I've always wanted this kind! What about buying it for my birthday?' Likewise, if a firm is finding more of its leads are coming from digital sources, they could expand that effort to capture where their audience is going.

Marketers of all stripes are tasked with understanding their own business strengths and concerns – moving to digital campaigns simply translates those needs into new channels of relationship with the customer.

Platform expertise and learning

Platform expertise is the hardest knowledge to keep evergreen, as technological channels go in and out of favour with the public. Still, there do tend to be key design themes and approaches that will serve the digital marketer well, regardless of tech *du jour*.

Digital marketing platforms primarily come in these flavours:

- customer relationship management (CRM) platforms (HubSpot, Pipedrive, Salesforce, Insightly and so on);[7]

- content management systems (CMSs) (Percolate, WordPress (free), Umbraco and so on);

- social or sharing platforms (Facebook, Twitter, Instagram, Pinterest and so on);

- social media management platforms – one level above the social platforms (Zoho Social, Hootsuite, HubSpot, Sprout Social and so on);[8]

- analytics platforms (often included with management platforms, Google Analytics, Crimson Hexagon, Synthesio and so on);[9]

- advertising platforms (Facebook, DoubleClick, Outbrain and so on).

Customer relationship management platforms

Customer relationship management platforms, or CRM systems, can help a business keep track of interactions with customers and, by so doing, increase the likelihood of closing a sale or successful marketing engagement.

CRM systems used to be centred around phone calls and postal mail; now CRM systems integrate with live chat and email systems, and even social media platforms.

The strength of CRM systems is their ability to collate data for analysis and even automate some functions, so that the business owner, salesperson or marketer can respond or initiate contact with customers in a smart way. Like all technologies, 'garbage in, garbage out' – if a business is not disciplined and consistent in updating contact information and transaction bookkeeping, having a CRM platform will not be particularly helpful to the marketer. Likewise, it may be that the measurements the CRM is set up to measure only tell part of the customer story, and the digital marketer may have to cross reference, say, sales reports, with marketing results captured in different analytics systems.

Content management systems

CMSs, once only the purview of newspaper or media websites, are now systems that help the enterprise. Because the greatest weapon in the digital marketing arsenal is useful content, and as the need for better, higher-quality content grows, one needs a place to create, review and store it – not to mention publish it!

Corporate bloggers used to need systems that would store created text, video, sounds, images and any other assets that they would link to from company blogs. Now CMSs also include workflow management (chain of approvals) and scheduling, often with a straight connection to the channel which they publish to (think company blog, YouTube channel and so on).

CMSs often have features that assist the administrators of such systems, for example, tools to change the appearance of a blog or timing when a blog post will appear. If this is a CMS that also publishes to the internet and maintains the presence of the content there (think WordPress, Blogger, Medium or other public article websites), it may also incorporate spam detection and blocking tools, anti-hacking features so that the administrator will be less worried about malevolent visitors to the published content. Some CMSs also incorporate multi-user options, so that the publisher of the content may enlist moderators to help handle the steady stream of comments from internet visitors.

Multimedia assets, such as infographics, podcasts, videos or made-to-order apps are often not created within the digital marketers' CMSs and are uploaded to the systems in order to publish them.

Multimedia assets have their own creator software and, for larger systems like musical composition or games, have their own asset management systems that may be separate from the digital marketers' CMS. Cloud storage systems, such as Dropbox, Microsoft OneDrive, Google Drive, WeTransfer, MailBigFile, MailDrop for Mac or Hightail (formally YouSendIt), are often the way that large-sized multimedia files get transferred from the agency or creator's computer to the one where the digital marketer is composing their campaign or publishing the company blog via a CMS.

Social or sharing platforms

Social or sharing platforms are software systems designed to promote or share content from users to each other. Generally, their features include:

- A profile with privacy or access settings, so that the user can control who sees their content and the projected identity of the user can be carefully crafted. That is, the user can select the best profile picture, the most socially flattering interests to go with their profile or even, in the case of LinkedIn, professional testimonials.

- A composing or editing feature, which allows the user to upload or create the content, edit it and then share it. Think about creating a board on Pinterest, applying Instagram filters to photos, editing a Facebook post and so on.

- Sharing functionality, controlled by the platform or by the user, which allows the user-created content to be seen, heard or shared by other users of the service, such as retweets on Twitter.

- For mature platforms with large user bases, a monetisation or advertising feature, which allows users to promote content of their choosing to others and pay for the privilege, or perhaps the platform itself charges users for the storage of larger multimedia items and so on.

These social channels and their advertising capabilities are central tools for the digital marketer, and technical skill as well as business observation will be key to using these platforms effectively.

For the sake of their career development, digital marketers should be on as many platforms as they can to test them out for the business.

Social media management platforms

Social media management (SMM) platforms, on the other hand, act one level above the social platforms. A business may have an online presence on multiple channels and need to get messaging out on all of them within a strict timeframe. SMM systems support the 'write once, publish many' necessities of digital marketing, as well as give integrated metrics tracking of how well the digital channels performed.

Analytics platforms

Metafilter and Slashdot are created by social media platform designers to keep people active on their services. These public displays of activity are like gold to the digital marketer, who can use that information to understand how well their message is getting across, and how loyal, satisfied or dissatisfied their online customers really are.

However, there may be times the digital marketer needs to go beyond the mechanisms of the social or sharing platform itself. For large-scale systems such as Twitter, where it is impossible for humans to keep up with the tweet stream, and only certain firms are licensed to use the data, doing sentiment analysis will need agency help or the use of a platform that has paid such licensing fees. Likewise, if you are trying to integrate metrics from several different platforms, a separate analytics service or platform may be what you need to bring it all together.

Analytics platforms should swiftly aggregate the findings from your campaigns in an easy-to-read format, offering visualisations and rollups so that the digital marketer can present a summary to executives or dig deeper into the data. The digital marketer should be wary of platforms that don't seem to measure the pertinent aspects of reaction to their campaigns or duplicate information that the digital marketer could learn from the social media platforms themselves. If the digital marketer can partner with a data scientist inside their firm, they may be able to tailor the analytics platforms to do deeper research studies around customer behaviour.

Advertising platforms

These platforms vary as much as the digital channels they serve, but here are a few of the more common types of advertising platforms, organised by how the customers perceive them.

Display or banner advertising networks
The most ubiquitous example of these for large companies and small proprietors would be Google AdSense or DoubleClick. These are ad-delivery and ad-placing systems for websites that track users and target for the benefit of their advertisers. Often, a customer is tracked by the placement of a cookie in their web browser, so that the advertising platform can figure out what the best advertisements to show this person are as they travel to sites that are part of the advertising network. If customers want to erase such tracking, they can opt out of the Google website or simply clear the cookies from their browser and browse incognito.

For the digital marketer, using an online advertising platform that allows targeting of users helps to make campaigns more effective. If the user is a regular on skiing websites for example, it makes sense to send them advertising relative to that sport rather than another, such as tennis. This is called contextual targeting, and it needs analysis of both the website hosting the ad and the keywords chosen by the digital marketer that best represent the kind of topics their customers are interested in.

Search engine advertising platforms
Search engine marketing is the advertisement of your company's product, web presence, landing page or other marketing target at the top of search engine results.

While there may be multiple consulting or agency approaches to this style of marketing, the technical understanding of this area is centred around the search engine itself and the tools the search engine provides for the creation and targeting of those ads. For Bing and Google, search engine marketing relies on the digital marketer choosing the appropriate search terms or keywords and this then leads to the presentation of the marketer's ad when the user queries in relation to those keywords.

A key aspect of search engine ad buying is that it is an auction – that is, the digital marketer decides upon desired keywords and how much to pay for a campaign, and the placement of the ads depends on the search engine's ad platform algorithms to ensure a good fit. Because the delivery of ads is automated in this way, a digital marketer who is new to search engine marketing may want to experiment with smaller keyword buys before investing a large amount in a set number of keywords. Larger corporations often employ in-house search engine marketers who have specialised in this kind of marketing or consultants who can tell the company what kinds of buys to make.

Search analytics are provided by the search engines so that an advertiser can track how well their ad performed and how long it took before the ad budget was expended. Generally, search ads have tended to be text snippets with a single link to the company website, but search engines have experimented beyond this and may offer other variations, such as business addresses and other site links inside the text-based search ads.

Mobile advertising
The ability to advertise to someone on a mobile device will only become more important as time goes on. Mobile ads can take different forms:

- a mobile-ready version of the banner, display or text a laptop user would see;
- a push notification (SMS) that urges the user to click a link or call a number;
- an ad shown in-app while the user is playing a mobile game;
- an ad that takes the user to Google Play, iTunes or another store to get them to download a mobile app (that promotes the business or brand for example).

Because a user's phone is very personal to them and represents restricted screen real estate compared to a tablet or laptop, mobile advertising has been a difficult medium for digital advertisers to crack successfully. Streamlined content to support lower bandwidth travel, audience targeting and sponsored or embedded advertising approaches may work well here. Garnering word-of-mouth support from your customers – so that they are texting their friends to recommend your product instead of you sending ads – is always a powerful choice.

Email marketing
Despite various articles suggesting that chat software will replace email as a communications channel, so far email marketing remains a steady digital marketing avenue. Bloggers and businesses create email newsletters to better serve interested consumers.

Illegal email marketing arises particularly when an email pretends to be from one source but is actually from another, or tries to get the consumer to give up personal information under false pretences.

Video advertising
Like display ads, online videos may be used to get a business' message across. The cheapest mechanism, of course, is having the digital marketer's own video 'go viral' and be shared across the internet without having to pay for anything except the creation and hosting of the video (often hosting comes free too, such as uploading a video to YouTube).

Social platforms that support video ads may result in more engaged customers; Twitter in 2016[10] reported more customers remembered video ads vs. other kinds of advertising on its service. Videos can be as costly to produce as a Hollywood trailer or as cheap as editing hand-held video footage from an iPhone on a free trial of video editing software. The smart digital marketer will decide whether video watchers are part of their marketing target and proceed from there to learn the video advertising aspects of specific digital platforms.

The digital marketer will also need to keep abreast of ad video trends, as issued by the Interactive Advertising Bureau (IAB), Media Rating Council (MRC) and other industry standards bodies. As consumer behaviour adapts to current video-serving mechanisms and ad stitching techniques, there will be further opportunity to disrupt and innovate in this area.

Sponsored content
Sponsored content enables bloggers to talk about the products they love and get paid for it. Bloggers that receive money for posting content must be clear that the content is sponsored by a brand, to ensure the line between commentary and advertisement is clear. Readers can decide for themselves whether the blogger's opinion was unduly swayed by compensation.

Sponsored content may also run into more elaborate and costly formats like a video, app or online game. Ideally, the sponsored content is aligned with branding goals and business success metrics, with a call to action clearly stated in the content or enabled by the content (for example, a 'buy' button in an app) or a contest entry that is part of the online game. There are specific agencies and platforms that create interactive branded content. As with video marketing, the digital marketer must decide whether this approach will appeal to their customers.

In the United States, by Federal Trade Commission (FTC) regulation, as of 2009, all bloggers and social media actors must disclose their receipt of payment or of a free product when promoting or endorsing products or services. As an additional wrinkle, if you are an employee of a company saying 'I love [my company's product]' you need to disclose in your profile that you are an employee of the company.

Opting in and opting out

It is important for the digital marketer to be aware of customer opt in or out options. In UK law,[11] marketers must check if their customers 'want to be contacted by fax, phone, post or email and give them the chance to object'.

The law says that marketers must get explicit customer permission to send them promotional materials. This is called 'opt in'. Marketers must also make it easy for customers to opt out (usually by either sending 'STOP' to a text 'short number' or through the use of an unsubscribe link).

Marketers must also check that they are not contacting anyone who has asked not to receive calls, faxes or emails and who has registered with the Telephone Preference Service,[12] Facsimile Preference Service[13] or the Mailing Preference Service.[14] Marketers must pay for and download the data file of customers who have registered for each service to ensure that they are complying.

The United States law leans more toward providing mechanisms to support customers opting out rather than requiring opt in. Many businesses have voluntarily created systems that default to requiring the opt in. All email newsletters must provide a way for customers to unsubscribe, and the Controlling the Assault of Non-Solicited Pornography And Marketing Act (CAN-SPAM) of 2003 went as far as to detail the deletion of the customer within 10 days.

Individual states within the US may also regulate electronic contact and Washington State's[15] law also covers unsolicited text messages (permitted only by the carrier or if a person has consented to receive them). The digital marketer working in US or, indeed, any global markets would do well to research legalities beforehand as laws evolve rapidly as the technological landscape changes.

DIGITAL MARKETER RESPONSIBILITIES

Digital marketing is a wide field with a large variety of responsibilities for those working within it, depending somewhat on the type of marketing path an individual wishes to follow.[16]

If the digital marketer role focuses on marketing content, for example, they will need to create and upload copy and images for their organisation's website. They will need to write and send email marketing campaigns to a content schedule defined by the organisation's marketing strategy. They will also develop and integrate content marketing strategies for the company.

The **corporate digital marketer** may need to contribute to social media engagement and brand awareness campaigns, if it is part of their role, and help with paid media initiatives. This may mean that the marketer needs to liaise with digital advertising agencies or manage the in-house customer contact database and help with lead generation activities.

Creative campaign managers at digital agencies will need to design website banners and help with the design of web visuals for the client. Each campaign will need to have effective keywords researched and web statistics reported on a regular basis to the client.

Marketing analysts will need to provide accurate reports and analysis of campaigns to clients (if working for a digital agency) and in-house company managers (if working as an employee of a company) to demonstrate that campaigns had an effective return on investment (ROI). They might also have to focus on the results produced by web analytics software, which monitor the performance of client websites and make recommendations for improvement.

Marketing sales executives will need to be able to communicate with clients, manage their affiliate networks and affiliate partners and negotiate with media suppliers to achieve the best price for clients.

In this section we will look at key responsibilities for most digital marketers.

Cross-team collaboration

Digital marketers need to interact and collaborate with many teams and technologies, namely:

- marketing executives;
- external marketing channel platforms including video game ad platforms, mobile ad platforms, Twitter, Facebook, blogs and information outlets, Instagram, Google, Bing, streaming services and so on;
- internal marketing and communications teams;
- PR and editorial teams;
- paid influencers;
- unpaid influencers ('earned' reach) – community building to maximise opportunities;
- creative agencies.

Online brand development

Before the rise of online media, marketers had specific avenues and almost codified mechanisms for setting up brand. A marketer worked hard to create an iconic logo on all packaging or brochures; established corporate sponsorships and ads that showed to the local or national community what the company stood for (the Super Bowl ads, parade floats, radio show sponsorships for example). Messaging was tested with focus groups and quantitative studies on the phone or in person, and success was measured through catchy jingles adopted by the public or word-of-mouth adoption of the phrases promoted by the company.

Now, representing a brand has become more complicated. In addition to the company logo having to adapt to the channel (by how many pixels can your logo shrink before it does not work anymore? Does your logo look as good on the side of a van as on a Pinterest board?), the places where a brand might showcase itself have increased. Whereas before, a marketer could more tightly control how a brand presented its values and aesthetic, because channels were limited, now a viral adoption or skewering of your carefully chosen brand presentation happens outside your control. With consumers having video cameras and sound recording devices in their phones, and easy access to bandwidth that makes uploads easy, a brand must stay ahead of the pack to succeed.

Digital audiences in different markets may have radically different temperaments from their traditional counterparts. Countries that may be unreceptive to your brand in traditional channels may become more accepting of the message presented digitally. Careful audience testing as your brand goes global will be key to success here, and a keen eye for the technology and legal trends within national borders is essential.

For a personal brand in particular, the increased scrutiny that comes with the digital realm can feel invasively judgmental. Thick skin must be developed as a personal individual brand is developed online. Not everyone can like you in real life; in the online realm insults and negative feedback are all recorded, forever.

It can be tempting to lash out when someone criticises you or your company online but it is important to carefully consider the impact of such actions. Likewise, for a personal brand effort, the digital marketer must decide carefully what areas of personality simply will not get expressed online (for privacy, and work-life reasons) and what areas of personality are part of the crafted personal brand.

Personal branding online can be just as difficult or more so than creating corporate branding.

Additionally, note that, as observed by social media influencer and entrepreneur Tara Hunt in her Truly Social video blog,[17] social capital takes a long time to nurture.

A digital marketer may spend years hunting for and becoming active in relevant communities, building trust, gaining expertise and then being able to authentically promote the brand or product for the business. The digital marketer must put in the effort to reach out day after day, offering tips and help week after week, to lay the foundation for a strong community around the product or the brand. Chris Brogan, who wrote *Social Media 101: Tactics and Tips to Develop Your Business Online*,[18] urges marketers to create a human approach that can foster lasting relationships.

This tension of being 'on' as well as polite, authentic and helpful, as well as smoothly professional, is the proverbial high wire act of digital marketers.

Here are a few tips for digital marketers establishing on online brand:

- Establish boundaries – such as a minimum time to respond to messages, mental conditions under which you will not take on social media conflicts or issues (you might be tired, hungry, angry or not prepared to deliver a service during off-work hours) and so on.

- Use content mechanisms that allow you to think through and craft your presence carefully.

- Carefully consider the photos and videos you post – make sure that they project the right online image.

- Set up checks and balances even if you operate as a sole proprietor or independent contractor, that the digital channels have a mix of both mandated business announcements or customer support information, and commentary that your audience can appreciate as coming from you personally.

Content marketing

Content marketing is the production of content of interest to your brand's customers – in the digital world, this is usually through a company-owned channel (website, YouTube, blog, Instagram and so on) or sponsored channel such as Medium or ZDNet – and aims to keep people interested and engaged with the company outside buying something. Psychological studies[19] have been done proving that a person who accepts something from another – a favour, a sweet, some information – is much more amenable to reciprocating (purchasing) in the future. That implicit sense of obligation prompts your customer to think more favourably of you and your company.

Salespeople know that they cannot just call their potential customers in sales mode; they must have other things to talk about and other things to offer. If you are a helpful enterprise rather than one that wants something from them, they are more likely to buy from you. Content marketing, by providing helpful content and updating interested customers with the latest announcements, builds that ongoing friendly relationship.

Visual marketing

As a consumer of media and internet culture, it is hard to miss the profusion of multimedia formats used to express ideas: emojis, interactive visualisations, games, animated gifs, video and sound clips, and full-length how-to videos. Regular people as well as marketing professionals understand that to help people like content, it needs to be jazzed up or augmented in a way that hooks the attention of the viewer.

Visual marketing techniques are best employed when text or other non-visual techniques would be too cumbersome. For example, if the digital marketer wants to present a new design for a dress, it would make sense to display a person wearing the dress so that the customer understands at a glance how the dress fits and what kind of body the dress was designed for. Likewise, if a car company wants to show the smooth handling of a luxury car on the road, it is best to show the car navigating steep mountain turns against a brilliant cobalt sky, rather than recite a table of statistics about brake speeds.

Brands whose identity is deeply entwined with visual aesthetic – architects, fashion designers, electronics manufacturers and so forth, would do well to engage visual marketing techniques to convey that aesthetic without having to spell it out. Luxury vs. money-saving brands, leisurely experiences vs. time-saving ones – these can be expressed in the visual presentation of each brand's messaging. We are shaped by media perceptions and media biases, and visual cues can be a shorthand that gets the value proposition across without a word being said.

A 2016 survey by Venngage[20] of 300 US marketers found that more than 90 per cent of the marketers used visual content in over half of the articles they published. Infographics were the most engaged-with content (42 per cent) with charts and data visualisations second (26 per cent) and videos or presentations third (20 per cent). Ironically, stock photography, which was used most frequently by a third of the marketers surveyed, did less than stellar. From this survey, multiple US business news outlets predicted 2017 would see an even greater increase in visual assets in marketing campaigns.

For a good reference of web visual design and video, see the Webby Awards (https://www.webbyawards.com/) to discover what agencies are creating for their clients.

Obviously, the taste *du jour* of the public will change over time, so this can only be a partial list of the possible visual and audio formats one might encounter. But this list can give the digital marketer a good foundation from which to proceed.

Cisco reckons that by 2019 a massive 80 per cent of global internet consumption will be video content.[21] HubSpot reckons that nine out of 10 customers say that videos are helpful in their decision-making process, with 75 per cent of online video viewers interacting with an online video ad each month.[22]

Static images

Sometimes an image with a smattering of text says it all. Platforms like Instagram, Tumblr and Pinterest have made use of 'flat' images with astonishing effectiveness. Bloggers find that adding photos for visual interest keeps their readers coming back and are an essential staple for how-to articles like recipes or home repair. Cat pictures on the internet have gone through cliché and come back again.

Such images are often reduced in size or compressed so that they are lightweight when downloaded in a browser or a phone or chat client. Common web formats are PNG, GIF and JPG but future technologies may find us viewing files that are even more compressed and efficient.

If using cute imagery, try to ensure that the overwhelming tone of cuteness works with the marketing message and does not distract from it. There are many online resources documenting visual tools for use on the web.[23]

Infographics

Popularised by Mashable.com and other online media outlets, marketing agencies must now be able to produce pictorial and visual representations of facts and data in a way that charms their audience. Using techniques from graphic novels, cartoons, data visualisation and Edward Tufte's information dissemination principles,[24] these infographics can make data stick in the viewers' minds more readily than a table of dry statistics.

More ambitious infographics are interactive, forcing the user to take actions that reveal the information, or progress them in a journey of understanding to the message the marketer (or news outlet) is trying to relay.

Infographics have pitfalls however – they can oversimplify a complex issue, making the resulting impression untruthful, or they can be so fancy or lavish that the user doesn't attempt to engage with them. Data in an infographic must have a cited source to be credible, and often an infographic is only as accurate as that source.

Emojis

Used at first for email and then text messaging to express emotional content, emojis are a pictorial language that communicates complex ideas in a small picture. Emojis now are not limited to expressing smiley (or frowny) faces; they can be objects, actions or even animated to make their point. It is possible to create entire tweets or blog posts out of emojis for comic effect, but it's important to take great pains in the crafting. Without words, the message can be ambiguous in ways the digital marketer may not expect.

Emojis are useful for online channels where space is at a premium (such as SMS messaging and Twitter). They can present the marketer or the company as cool and humorous. But they must be handled sensitively; in 2017, *The Emoji Movie* marketers got into hot water by using emojis to satirise *The Handmaid's Tale* original TV series from Hulu.[25] The TV series would go on to win Emmys; *The Emoji Movie* made only $25 million in its first box office showing.

Animated GIFs or short-form looping videos

Animated GIFs first became popular in the 1990s when Netscape and then other web browsers were first able to support them. An animated GIF has multiple images embedded in the file that display in sequence. The compression of the GIF format allowed webmasters and other creators to catch the attention of viewers through movement and repetition.

The natively limited palette of GIFs makes them appropriate for certain messages, while other more complex messages may call for full video to obtain appropriate richness.

Short-form looping videos that autoplay (often silently) provide the same attention grabbing response from the public but with richer visual content. For the purposes of this discussion, short form is less than 15 seconds; for some it may be less than five. As 30 seconds is generally the point at which many viewers will leave a video, the shorter the format, the more chance the digital marketer has of landing the message.

Social curation and storytelling applications

Storify is an application that allows the user to capture social media posts such as Twitter, Facebook and Instagram and assemble them into narrative formats, timelines or stories. News organisations have used Storify to capture public reaction to events, and online commentators will often capture their own tweetstorms or series of posts in a 'storified' format to offer the narrative all in one place.

At the time of writing, Storify is part of Adobe's online publishing offering, and falls under the category of social media management software. Familiarity with it is extremely useful for the digital marketer.

Pinterest boards

These represent another form of visual, social curation and have been used by brands and consumers alike with remarkable success. The highly visual assembly of 'pins', coupled with links to the content, act as visual marketing for the creator's personal brand as well as marketing for the products inside the pins. Without its high emphasis on visual richness, Pinterest as a social sharing platform would never have grown as it has. Digital marketers should watch this and other such highly visual social platforms with interest, to determine what new techniques they may best employ.

Podcasts

Commuting to work, working out at the gym, waiting in line at the post office – these are ripe times for a consumer to be listening to or watching your podcast. As mobile phones become a staple of modern life, portable internet shows that can be downloaded, then turned on and off at leisure, are a way to fill boring spaces in a day or learn new skills while doing something else.

Digital marketers creating podcasts have some of the same requirements as long-form video creators (see the next section); that is, if you are going to take up minutes of someone's time, the information content cannot be shallow, and it must be worth their time. Discussions of thorny business problems, sequences of how-to steps or tutorials, or witty hosts with entertaining banter taking up topics your customers are interested in – these are all good formulas for podcasts that people will download.

Long-form videos

Movie trailers that tease fans and critics alike with excerpts and action are one example of how long-form video works well for digital marketers. However, there are other approaches that can work whether the digital marketers are representing only themselves as consultants or presenting the messaging of a larger company.

360-degree videos

Estate agents and hoteliers have long understood the power of the 360-degree video in attracting customers; it may be that if your firm's wares or services are best shown as a surround, as a digital marketer, you will want to make use of these technologies.

Live videos

Live videos are changing the digital landscape. Social media platforms such as Facebook, Instagram, Snapchat and Twitter with Periscope use live video to capture the customer's attention. Facebook apparently ranks live videos higher than other content in its newsfeed.[26]

Vlogging

With the rise of YouTube and other video hosting sites, video blogs have become a new form of internet television. Digital marketers can use their video channels to create engaging long-form content on a regular basis, like video blogger Gary Vaynerchuk who promoted his family's wine business from $4 million to $60 million.[27]

How-to videos

From home repair, IKEA furniture assembly to video game walkthroughs, how-to videos can be highly lucrative for the creator and for the advertiser who wants to appeal to a niche audience. How-to videos lend themselves easily to segmentation, and can (like the video blogging approach) create an internet celebrity if well done.

Good camera work exposing the nuances of how to do something is often essential to the success of a how-to video, but it does not have to be entirely serious. Sometimes the how-to video can be tongue in cheek and still go viral (such as the Blendtec 'Will it blend' series of blender destruction).[28]

Channel understanding and selection

Channel selection for a digital campaign will depend on the channels available to the digital marketer, in terms of opportunity and budget. In thinking about which channels to use, the digital marketer must carefully consider the goals of their campaign and then ensure the channels align with those goals.

All marketing campaigns, particularly digital ones, must contend with the scarcity of user attention. With the explosion of internet content, and a device in every pocket, the average consumer does not need the addition of another marketing campaign to distract them further – they have enough to pay attention to already. This then is the challenge of picking the channel – how to best capture and win potential customers over to the brand or product in a way that does not allow them to resent you for doing so.

Timing is key; when strategising a marketing campaign, it is important to note which messages are likely to be delivered real time, in response to customer actions, and which will be seen asynchronously – that is, at some indeterminate time after the content is sent out (think about how little control a digital marketer has over whether a user checks email hourly, daily or weekly, if at all).

On the other hand, a pop-up ad or dialogue box in response to a user action creates more of a contextual link between message and user frame of mind.

If advertising to millennials, for example, the digital marketer would do well to look at visual content, fast-moving approaches and channels that might overwhelm older generations who are not digital natives. Hashtags, animated GIFs, photographic filters, emojis – these are all signals that the creator is listening to the trendiest online conversations and the marketer needs to pick channels where these signals come across.

Table 2.1 shows an example of both asynchronous and real-time channels used to deliver messages to readers.

If budget permits, the digital marketer would do well to create a pilot campaign or test run on the selected channels to see how well their message lands. For example, the company creates a how-to blog for people using its power tools – look at how many views that blog post gets. The company tweets a dozen discount codes – how quickly are they snapped up? Watching how the results come in to the pilot can help a digital marketer make the decision of whether to commit more marketing spend to that channel or take the money and put it into a different channel.

The other side of the equation, as the marketer is considering which channels to use, is how the prospective customer will be handled once the message is presented. For instance, it

Table 2.1 Asynchronous vs. real-time activities

Asynchronous channels	Real-time channels
User does not have to be present at the time of broadcast to gain access to the message:	User must be signed in, present and perform an action for the marketer to reach them:

Asynchronous channels	Real-time channels
<ul><li>blogs;</li><li>microblogs (Tumblr, Instagram);</li><li>downloadable podcasts and vlogs;</li><li>Pinterest and other visual curation sites;</li><li>Facebook;</li><li>YouTube;</li><li>Storify;</li><li>email newsletters.</li></ul>	<ul><li>live-streamed events and webinars;</li><li>sponsored online games;</li><li>live chats or Reddit 'Ask Me Anything' (AMA) sessions;</li><li>tweets (unless captured in Storify or other asynchronous medium);</li><li>search engine marketing (user must actively do a search to see these ads);</li><li>online ad networks (user must be actively browsing to a page to get these ads);</li><li>interactive infographics;</li><li>in-app advertising (mobile games).</li></ul>

is hard to create a TV spot that links to your website (though with more consumers playing with phones and tablets as they watch TV, it is possible for them to pick up your URL with more speed than it was five years ago).

A customer driving to work and listening to the radio may not have hands free to remember a long URL to your landing page, so keep it brief. Ideally use a memorable phrase that is included in your domain name or something they could punch into a search engine and find your website with.

Facebook ads may link to a Facebook app, a company's Facebook page or off the Facebook domain entirely into the digital marketer's blog. Promoted tweets with a shortened URL used to only have 140 characters to explain themselves, so, ideally, they would link to a landing page with more content and more appealing text. Even Twitter's 280-character limit is not a lot of space to get a message across.

Pinterest boards can age, so provide an alternative product like Nordstrom does – if the pin links to something out of stock, the Nordstrom site offers other choices immediately as if the item no longer exists.

If a user gives up their email address for your newsletter, then the newsletter had better have a great subject line, and its body copy better be entertaining and full of content to retain interest. Ensure that the call to action is immediate ('Sale ends today!' for example).

For real-time campaigns, the user is present and engaged with the digital content or an influencer representing the company or brand. Here, the handoff is just as important, but the feelings of immediacy, authenticity on the part of the brand and clear utility must be paramount. If your campaign's appeal is making it possible for that customer to interact with one of their heroes, then ensure that the hero or influencer is conversing with as many customers as possible. If the expert teaching the webinar can field questions from the live audience, attendees will feel they have gotten value for their most priceless currency: time. In-the-moment, emotional experiences can create powerful feelings of loyalty and advocacy for customers and the savvy digital marketer tells a story and creates that experience with real-time approaches. Beautiful interactive graphics and powerful game mechanics with humour or insightfulness from the company that sponsored them will create strong memories and bring users back to your online presence.

Coordinating asynchronous with real-time approaches

The good news here is that many real-time experiences can be archived or re-packaged as asynchronous content. So, for the thousands of users who cannot take time off from work to attend your webinar or who missed the notification of the influencer's live-streamed demo of your product, recordings and transcripts can be made for the people that follow along later.

Often, the transcripts or recorded video clips end up having more views or usage than the initial presentation, simply because it could only happen at one time for the first time and there are many hours and days that follow. Therefore, it is important in the moment of the real-time event or engagement that the users who made the time to attend are made to feel special by the brand or company. Anyone on the internet can read the Storify or the chat transcript. But only a few will have the experience of being answered by a tastemaker seconds after they tweet her, or crafting a question that helps others to solve a difficult business problem.

So, for a webinar, the campaign may be broken into several phases: pre-event promotion, where the webinar's date and time are made known to the public, event promotion on the day for last-minute attendees to push the immediacy, and then post-event promotion of artefacts like the transcripts or recorded clips, to catch folk unable to join online at the designated moment. The digital marketer must think of the value to the customer at each stage of this process, and how to best present the digital experience in each phase.

Case Study: TED Talks

As an example of such integration, TED talks in 20-minute video clip format are seen all around the world, and TED thoughtfully provides transcripts on their website, Ted.com. The 20-minute talks are long enough to be of substance, short enough that someone could watch on their lunch break and are technologically created to be shared globally.

Thousands of people experience TED through these recordings and transcripts or hear broadcast versions through the TED radio hour on public radio. As the TED organisation's mission centres around 'ideas worth spreading' their goal is that any one TED talk may have years of enjoyment by the public.

On the real-time side, TED attendees gladly pay $10,000 USD (at the time of writing) to be in the same food queues as the speakers and be part of the audience for the first-ever, live talk as it is given. Attendees come back year after year to be there in person because the event organisers work hard to create an experience that matters on site as well as in retrospective views of the talks, and curate the attendees' experience to ensure random chats in the coffee bar with speakers will be possible.

Knowing that the ticket cost of this experience is out of reach for many, TED promotes community TED talks via TEDx organisers who create local opportunities for great live speeches and recorded talks. Meticulous policies around the way the TEDx licence holder creates the experience ensures that the local TEDx is as much like the larger TED experience as possible. Through the TED conference itself attracting global industry giants, celebrities and scientists (think influencers) and its footprint of recorded content and home-grown events local to each community, the TED brand has global reach. Even better, it has an experience or product for everyone, from the free online videos to the costly chance to bump into Bill Gates in the corridor.

Working with influencers and cultivating them

An influencer in the digital marketing world is someone who attracts attention and has followers they can activate around their comments, issues or causes. It may be a traditional media celebrity, whose sense of style, performance and aesthetic has captured the attention of many people who want to emulate them. It may be someone who works in the business area of your product and is looked upon as a guru or tastemaker when it comes to this area of product or skillset. Often these people are charismatic extroverts – online, if not in person – and their cultivated personas online are ones that have the potential to elevate your brand.

Whether a digital marketer ends up paying the influencer to represent the product depends on that topic area and the relationship the influencer has with the marketer's company already. If the influencer is a woodworking enthusiast, for example, and has created many how-to videos using the brand's tools, they may already be working to promote sales of the woodworking tools without a formal relationship. Authentic endorsement and knowledge in this instance is more powerful than a paid relationship as it has risen organically, and the viewers of such videos will not feel the influencer's endorsement is tainted by monetary interest.

On the other hand, digital marketers pushing products around mothers and children, for example, will probably have to pay for the privilege of appearing on a popular mommy blog in the United States, or to be featured in a newsletter, Instagram or Pinterest board around that topic.

Women often control much of the budgetary purchasing power in UK and American households; digital marketers promoting their own brand as mothers command a high premium because they can activate their followers with their own experiences.

Table 2.2 shows how paid and unpaid campaigns can affect an audience.

Table 2.2 Campaign impact on audience

Audience impacts		
Paid outreach	Ineffective	Effective
	(Perhaps you paid the wrong influencer or they were turned off by the sponsored relationship)	(Your intended audience trusts this influencer, even when products are sponsored)
Unpaid outreach	Ineffective	Effective
	(You got what you paid for – low reach, low ability to move audience to action)	(Influencer was a natural advocate and didn't require payment to endorse your product, leading to a more authentic following)

In the United States, bloggers must show that they have been paid for a blog post that endorses a product.

Identifying influencers

Digital marketers first have the difficult job of identifying who the internet celebrities are, particularly if the audience segment being targeted is one that has not been part of the company's customer base before. They can look for obvious signs of influence like follower counts and shares, seeing how much of the influencer's base is responding to the new content being published by the influencer. They can research if the influencer has been used by a competitor (which has pros and cons) to endorse a similar product. And they can see if the influencer already is a friend to their product or brand organically (best of all), so it is not a far step for the influencer's fan base to see them working with that company or brand.

Fame is different from activation. Many people may follow celebrities to see when the next concert is, or because they want to hear what the celebrity is doing, but would baulk at switching their favourite brand of toothpaste just because the celebrity said so. By filtering and sifting through online personalities, never forget that the digital marketer is sifting for their audience and to see if that base could be a good set of potential customers. The online personality may be a magnetising force for people of like-mind, but if these like-minds do not interact with each other as well as the influencer, there may not be enough of an actual community there to leverage.

Online forums, Facebook groups and other online common spaces are ways to find communities of like-minded potential customers. Once they adopt your product or brand as part of their identity, they will sell your product for you (observe how the rise of CrossFit gyms in the US had a parallel Paleo diet craze cropping up with them, and subsequently Paleo diet products[29]). Guy Kawasaki, Apple's first product evangelist who set a trend for the industry, has long promoted tapping into customers' passion as a mainstay of digital marketing. In the 1980s, he created a community of people who loved Apple products and went on to consult and write books about creating relationships with customers as the real secret to marketing success.

Knowing then, that the influencers you would like to woo, or employ, are interested in fostering relationships with their audience, and in promoting themselves as authentic champions of good things, the digital marketer must not only look at follower and brand fit but also the personality of the influencer. For example, if their online persona includes swearing and your brand is more tempered in speech, while they may have earnest followers who love the plain talk — having them represent your product or brand may not work well. If the influencer endorses 20 products each week, with minimal attention to a cohesive narrative or how those products fit his or her online identity, their personality may be too diluted or broad to promote your product.

To get away from broad appeal influencers who cannot mobilise their audience, digital marketers may then turn to micro-influencers. These are online personalities, with perhaps several thousand followers or more, who have tuned their content stream to communities and themes, for example: beauty, sport or technology. It takes more work to find these themed experts but they are working harder to appeal to their constituency. Coordinating multiple micro-influencers to endorse your product may be more cost-effective than paying for one heavy hitter celebrity who has no native interest in your products.

Celebrity tweets or other endorsements by Hollywood stars are paid as you would expect – in the thousands or millions of dollars. Social media behaviours would be included as part of the contract your firm would write and are as carefully negotiated as other performance measures.

The digital marketer as an influencer

If the digital marketer is fortunate enough to build their online presence such that they themselves are an influencer, they may, like Guy Kawasaki, need help to keep their audience fed and happy. For Kawasaki's start-up Alltop, he regularly promoted content and stories found by his assistants and his star quality ensured that the links would be shared on Twitter and elsewhere. He posted the content that passed his review multiple times in one day, and his team became the engine behind all the insightful shared links. Kawasaki, who has sat on multiple boards and founded several companies, does not have time to research everything on the internet. He used his personal brand, then, to promote Alltop and online content he deemed worthy.

A team to manage your company's social media channels needs careful coordination by the digital marketer. Timing to get the message across multiple social platforms, ensuring that content assets are present when they are due to be published, and that firestorms or controversies arising from the social channels are handled promptly, is essential. These teams may fall under a director of marketing or, if a vendor team, under a marketing manager that would run several such campaigns with help.

Holding an influential position on a social media channel needs discipline and upkeep, being careful to stay on-brand and in a mode of utmost kindness to your audience. Internet personalities are forced to grow thick skins, and it may be difficult for some traditional marketers who are not used to the public eye to adjust to negative reactions in the beginning. However, naysayers or 'haters' are expected if one has an online leadership position or has taken a position on an issue. Gracious behaviour on the part of the digital marketer, with an eye toward personal security and the reputation of the business, will go a long way toward defusing trolls. Blocking or banning an abusive customer from your company's community outreach area is a valid defence, especially if that person is seen abusing your other customers as well as the online brand representative.

Community management

Community management is a responsibility some digital marketers may have. Long before the rise of social media, tech companies had online forums for customers to pose questions and get answers from company representatives – Microsoft and Dell being larger-scale examples – and they would hire or assign employees to manage the community around their products and services.

Now, Amazon has forums for consumers to post information about using Amazon vendors' products, and other consumer sites around coupon codes and promotional information –

in short, a community may spring up around your product whether you want it to or not.

One way to control that discussion – or at least provide an official channel by which the satellite communities might get information – is for a company to host their own community area and hire digital marketers known as community managers to serve as hosts and support it. There are business advantages to creating your own, branded space. If Facebook shut down your Facebook page, how would you communicate with customers? If Twitter goes out of business, would you lose all ways of connecting to that audience?

Community management skills go beyond banning users for bad conduct, enforcing terms of service and posting the latest sale updates on the forum. These digital marketers, in addition to possessing brand skills, really must think about member acquisition and measurement of engagement within the company's community area. They must consider why a customer would come to them instead of the company's Facebook page, Twitter account or other social means.

Often, as with the Microsoft and Dell examples earlier, the company-hosted areas were mainly used for customer support. Rather than paying for a bank of telephone customer service reps answering duplicate questions, having an online repository of focused questions and answers allows a user to solve their problem without waiting on the phone. Companies are expected to be the foremost experts on those kinds of problems and some credibility can be lost by having an influencer repeat 'how to debug' instructions. So, as the digital marketer thinks about growing the company's user base – and the community conversations around the company's products – they would do well to think about whether the company could use its own hosted community area for directly relating to customers.

Useful skills for digital marketers tasked with community management are:

- Mastering acquisition – Know how to use CRM tools for email newsletters, sales calls and social media to shepherd customers into your company's community forum.

- Establishing identity – What does being in your company's tribe represent? Do you offer giveaways or badges or other signs of appreciation from company to customer? Items that grassroots community leaders can hand out to their constituents?

- Establishing conduct – What societal rules are needed for your company's community spaces? What measures do you have to defuse conflict or moderate or ban abusive members? Community managers must often work in tandem with company legal services (and know local laws) around what a company can be sued for, or not sued for, pertaining to community forums they sponsor.

- Grassroots activation – Get your customers to promote your company. Sponsoring most-valued-professional (MVP) programmes (where special community leaders within your forum are given special previews or discounts so they can show others your latest offering) can often help in getting the word out beyond the company-hosted community.

- Knowing when to stop focusing on a product line or website (sometimes known as its 'sunset'), deprecate or retire a community – Perhaps the beloved product is no longer being made by the company. Maybe the community, despite best moderation practices, became overrun by trolls. Maybe the company cannot afford to support the servers and moderation costs to allow the community to function. Regardless of the reason, a community manager knows when it is time to close the community doors and focus on another area of digital marketing.

Search engine optimisation (SEO) and marketing

Like the possibilities presented by digital technologies, search engine marketing is always changing. Google, Bing,

Yahoo, DuckDuckGo and others will continually adjust their algorithms, seeking to improve the quality of their search results. For search engine companies, there is a never-ending arms race against spammers and junky content farms that seek to game the system and sell ads on websites that have little of value on them (but get all the search result clicks). There is always a better way to serve search ads atop or amidst search results, improving them visually or in regards to relevance, and constant vigilance is needed to ensure that malware pushers or bad actors do not appear in the advertisements.

For the digital marketer, SEO and search engine marketing (SEM) are likewise an arms race of content, ad spend and strategic technical construction. Clear and useful content organised in easy-to-read hierarchies is the first order of business. Even if a business never buys any ads, its content quality can drive it to be organically ranked among the first and most-desired search engine results.

Content quality

Overall content quality has been touted by all search engines as the recipe for placing higher in search results.

Clear and useful content is not always easy to create. Basics such as including your firm's physical address, phone numbers and daytime hours help search engines in creating instant 'answers' on the page that highlight info you want customers to see. Concise descriptions of what your firm does and does not do, and presenting front-and-centre each benefit or value proposition of your services seems simple, yet many businesses looking to wow people with flowery phrases or important-sounding language often end up confusing both customers and search engines with their prose.

This attention to content quality goes beyond the home page. Each 'Contact Us' page, each product detail page, each online form that encourages a user to sign up for a newsletter or online seminar must engage and inform in a way both potential customers and search engines can read. Sometimes frequently asked questions (FAQ) pages, often written as an afterthought of useful extras that didn't make it into the other pages, can be the most popular page of the site. Make sure that your FAQ page contains your branding message!

Hyperlinks

Interspersed with content strategies for a business website is the strategy around hyperlinks, or simply 'links'. A site's trustworthiness as a valid destination (vs. the so-called 'link farm') is based on the inbound links to it. (A link farm is a website created to link to your main website. The outbound links will supposedly increase standing with Google or other search engines.) If, say, *The New York Times* in an article links to the website, the site is more valid than a website with no inbound links, or links from sites created recently with no trustworthy inbound links of their own. A digital marketer should analyse whether other pages on the internet link to the company website(s), or discover if they are siloed, cut off from possible organic web traffic.

The choice of outbound links matters a bit less, though outbound links can help to prove in customer eyes what part of the digital conversation your business is maintaining. For example, a knitting business might link to classes or locations where someone can buy the best wool.

Internal links, however, are key for search engines to understand the hierarchy of your site and drive traffic to pages underneath the home page. Search engines deploy automated bots, or crawlers, that go through every page of every site, following the links within it. Well-structured websites that have proper links to sub-pages help to keep those pages in context and can also be highlighted by search engines when they display your website in their results.

Alt. tags

Within the body of a web page, in its HTML code, are provisions for displaying images and video files. Because a search engine reads text primarily, these multimedia files are not 'searched' the way a web page would be. If you want to ensure search engines understand anything about the multimedia you offer on the page, ensure the caption and surrounding text indicate what it is. Then, use the Alt. attribute in the HTML code (also known as an 'Alt. tag' or 'Alternative tag') to add further contextual information for search engines and for accessibility purposes.

Best practices for Alt. tags include:

1. If clicking on an image takes a user to a link, include that link in the text within the Alt. tag, or 'Alt. text'.
2. Use spacing within the Alt. tag to ensure readability, and keep it under 125 characters to support accessibility.
3. If you have a complex chart or video it may be best to summarise rather than link to a separate page that spells out the content of the multimedia (and derailing the user from the page they were just reading).

An example of Alt. tag or Alt. text usage is:

```
<img src="EileenBrown.gif" alt="Eileen Brown
speaking at a conference in London">
```

This is an image HTML tag. The 'source of the image' (SRC) is listed as the gif's name; on a website most likely it would be the URL where that image is hosted.

Regarding website construction, a digital marketer should be technical enough to understand the underpinnings of website pages beyond just Alt. tags. This is outside the scope of this book, but we recommend learning more about HTML, CSS and even some JavaScript to understand what the search engine crawler encounters when it tries to make sense of your website.[30]

Other considerations

A digital marketing strategy around SEO will have to consider many technical details of websites. Are the pages dynamic or static (search engines read these pages differently)? Are keywords or other metadata properly positioned inside the HTML to help indicate (beyond the visible text of the page itself) what category the business falls within? Is the page using schema.org-recommended schema markup, so that the business controls more of what text snippets appear under its search result links?

Do the websites (or suite of websites) supporting the business offer, as part of their directories, well-defined and updateable XML sitemaps? Are the XML sitemaps registered properly with the search engines? Bing[31] and Google[32] both maintain webmaster resources to help site owners navigate this landscape (and not so coincidentally, lead them to advertising resources).

When considering search advertising, it is useful to consider exactly how consumers use search engines. They type in a few words and expect magic to appear shortly after in the form of carefully tailored results built somehow on that word choice (voice search is another topic, but the result is the same – the machine must understand what the human is saying or typing based on word choice).

A helpful place to begin is to look at what searches are driving traffic to the business site currently (both Google and Bing have tools and consoles to help you do this in their webmaster and advertising resources). What words are the consumers associating with your business when they arrive at your site and what words are the search engines deciding you should be aligned with? What search terms are best for the business to be associated with and are any missing?

That is why search engine advertising revolves around keywords, those text choices made by users typing into text boxes or shouting into the hardware of their personal assistant. There is power in having your carefully tailored ad show up in the topmost result for one of those words, and having the customer delighted when clicking through that the site does everything he or she wants. It does not do any good for a business to be associated with a popular search term like 'Facebook' – if the business is not Facebook.

As keyword popularity is driven by the consumers themselves, it is a never-ending requirement to keep up. Slang usage, hot topics, peaking memes inform the language of marketing but also of ad words targeting. In search ad spending, the digital marketer must watch current keyword rates and the language around their industry's customers to stay atop of fresh search trends.

Designing metrics of success and understanding current metric standards

For digital marketers on a budget, metrics of success will be determined by the products they are able to use to test effectiveness and that align to industry standards.

Social platforms themselves, to encourage social exchanges, often present even consumers with analytics data that can be used to understand effectiveness ('this post got 50 "likes" from your Facebook friends', for example).

A fairly new skill for digital marketers is the design of new metrics based on what is offered by digital platforms, such as Google Analytics, in conjunction with their business goals.

If they have a new digital product to launch, this may mean additional attributes added to the product to enhance what they can understand from analytics around the behaviour of users. For example, a video game developer may instrument their mobile application so that they can track how many times a user saw the upsell icon within the game and decided not to click on it.

The instrumentation of the landing page where those customers first encounter the marketer's product may be able to approximate page duration until the product buy button is clicked. Or, if the product itself is digital, it may be able to detect when a customer comes in through a marketing campaign by offering a different download or signup flow to help the digital marketer keep track. Creating this will usually be beyond the technical skill of the digital marketer but they will need to recognise when they hit the brick wall of 'I want to know X, but the current tracking systems do not provide it for me' and work with their technical colleagues or staff to improvise or find better methods of tracking customers.

Organisational communication

The previous chapter discussed the outward-facing communications that the digital marketer has with customers and potential customers. But there is another audience for the digital marketer that is ignored at your peril: the stakeholders of the business who want to understand how the company's relationships with the customers or the public have improved.

The digital marketer is always moving quickly to inform multiple stakeholders of what is happening in each digital campaign, and should set up both templated status reports and recurring meetings to discuss each phase of the campaign with those who require this information.

Communication with stakeholders varies depending on whether the digital marketer is alone (an independent consultant, for example) or part of an agency supporting a business client, or if the digital marketer is in-house and an employee of the firm requiring the marketing support.

Agency communication

Agency communications with customers and also internal cross-team communication depend on the size of the client and the agency. Dealing with a large, international organisation focused across industries requires a different dynamic than dealing with a customer focused in one country and one industry. Therefore, agencies need to consider the following:

- External communications with the client should keep the client abreast of progress, but not expect them to solve problems internal to the agency.
- Internal resourcing discussions, problems with the project calendar and collaboration on deliverables

within the agency should be resolved away from the client so that the client experience is smooth and professional and the reputation of the agency isn't damaged.

- Status, metrics and honest discussion of problems or successes will be paramount.

External interactions with clients will often fall into this structure:

1. Informational meeting(s) with the client to understand need, scope of project and what the client's definition of success is.
2. Internal agency proposal generation – creating a business proposal or statement of work that the client can evaluate in terms of tactics and costs to determine if they would like to employ the agency.
3. Iterating the statement of work until components of a contract are finalised. It's important to discuss pricing.
4. Client and agency sign contract, releasing digital marketer or agency resources to work on behalf of client.
5. Kick-off meeting to establish rhythm of subsequent meetings and checkpoints. Some projects may require daily check-ins; others may require a weekly sync between digital marketer and client.
6. If the scope of work changes (either by the client deciding to use the agency for more campaigns, or the agency discovers that the contract won't cover all the work needed), meetings will be needed to hammer out the amendments to the contract and extra work.
7. At each phase of the campaign, the client may require metric reporting (on a live campaign) or reports of progress (if producing creative or other assets).

8. As the campaign winds down, the digital marketer should be able to create a summary report listing the outcome of the campaign, the actions taken by the brand or the agency and (if the client is amenable) proposals for subsequent work or directions to take the campaign.

9. Should anything go awry with the campaign, the digital marketer or agency will be expected to notify the client, possibly offering makegood services or collateral, in a manner dictated by the contract or business relationship.

Communication should take the format preferred by the client. So, if the client prefers a weekly videoconference do that. If they want items sent to an email or cloud storage location do that. At all times the communications are considered business confidential and are not to be shared by the digital marketer with any other party, without the client's permission. Taking pains to create secure storage locations or password-protected web locations where creative assets might be tested will help to keep client information and future marketing plans secure.

Internal agency communications will fall under the company culture and policy of that agency. However, just as the external client needs metric reports and status emails about how the project is doing, so will the management of the agency who are keeping an eye on billable hours and not spending more resources or time on a contract than is specified.

Corporate communication

Inside a large corporation, the in-house digital marketer will also be bound by company protocols. However, they should keep in mind that their own management chain must not be unpleasantly surprised by any action or direction the campaign is taking, and that it is a courtesy to ensure that one's boss or executive sponsor is not surprised by any marketing development.

This may mean information passing from marketing coordinators up through their managing director or vice president, with excerpts and key statistics included in each report (condensed in final form for executive or board reviews). But it may also mean preparing presentations from one's own department to other departments, reliant on who has a say in how the marketing campaign is executed – sales, engineering, finance, accounting, legal, other account managers, directors and so on.

Regular working meetings with digital marketing teammates will ensure that work is progressing as agreed in the initial brief. Weekly meetings with stakeholders and other corporate customers will, at minimum, keep the team abreast of campaign progress and setbacks during its lifetime.

If marketing responsibilities are split across several teams – perhaps one team does digital, another does broadcast, television or radio advertising, and a third does events and sponsorships, setting up a regular meeting where the integration points of the separate campaigns can be discussed is critical. This is where the digital marketer's project management and drive for results comes into play, as timing, content and budget may come from sources external to the digital team. It is important that the communications be collaborative, as the company will win only if all facets of marketing work together.

Keeping up to date with technical trends and new digital platforms

Digital marketers need to keep up with technology news – as presented in technology-only news outlets such as *Geekwire, TechCrunch, The Register, VentureBeat, Wired*, and *ZDNet*. Underneath all the stories of start-up failure and acquisition, you gain a sense of the bleeding edge's adoption rate and fresh marketing opportunities. Google Glass, for example, was a flop as a consumer product but a win in the early tech adopter community and is now re-purposed toward industrial, commercial and enterprise use, attracting business-to-business customers. One could see, in the on-the-ground reaction to the wearers of the product, who were called 'Glassholes' by some, that a marketing campaign flowing only through those spectacles was an idea whose time had not yet come. Not that the day for its success will never come – just that it might not have paid off at that moment to invest in that line of digital marketing research.

Virtual reality (VR) and augmented reality (AR) promise new open spaces for digital marketers to exploit in the future. Facebook's latest exploration of virtual spaces (aptly named Facebook Spaces) suggests that the social network giant does not want to be left out of this arena. Amazon has been staffing in VR, and entertainment companies such as Netflix and Hulu are working on the next-generation VR apps.

QR codes, which are a cheaper form of digital AR already in use, allow a user's phone to access a customised experience by having the phone camera view the code. This offers the digital marketer opportunity to offer customised discounts. More elaborate AR marketing might take the shape of a game – think of an immersive scavenger experience, such as Pokémon Go, where the customer travels to different stores to build up loyalty points or prizes, or receives cumulative discounts the more they shop and 'play'.

Self-driving cars likewise have captured the tech industry's imagination, and they offer opportunities to market to customers. Much as New York City cabs have in-cab entertainment and promotional messaging, it is easy to imagine a fleet of autonomous cars offering ads in response to the traveller's destination. Global positioning system (GPS) tracking is pinpoint geomarketing, and in understanding a driver's habitual routes the digital marketer could offer incentives to get them off the beaten path, or tailor special offers for particular products in those shops and restaurants on their regular routes.

Quantified self-movement devices, such as heart rate monitors and sleep sensors, may be another kind of opportunity to the digital marketer. As the consumer tracks their own health journey, you might be able to time product offerings or services to customer ability and aspirations. Meal tracking apps are a staple of diet regimens, and a logical place for the well-positioned product to make a pitch. Digital marketing works best when the audience tracking makes it possible to only give customers what they would want. As you evaluate trends where consumers are gladly giving up information for services in return, think about how that self-selection works and how you might use that self-selection to target those who would be receptive to your message.

Platforms like Pinterest, which functions as a highly visual, social-self-expression mechanism, further help you to understand the tastes and desires of the potential audience. A creator who compiles large boards of Star Wars collectibles has signalled their aesthetic and their interest. The people who choose to view their boards share that mindset and propensity to be interested in ideas aligning with those interests. Big corporate brands want to be present on Pinterest as a channel for business communication. But the digital marketer of the future looks at self-expression mechanisms like Pinterest and Facebook for the social signals they allow consumers to emit and marketers to gain insights from.

Disaster planning and emergency PR measures

Traditional marketers had to worry about glitches in broadcast advertisements or press backlash against a campaign, but these tended to be crises handled within normal business hours. With the 24 hours a day, seven days a week nature of online media, and the way conversations about products and brands have become truly global in scope, a digital marketer does not have the same luxury that the marketer of earlier days had.

While many PR firms or departments handle launch days or big announcements with contingency planning, the digital marketer needs to set up techniques, messaging and escalation or decision paths before entering digital channels.

If there is a problem with a video clip, the digital marketer needs to have the agency contacts or the technique and knowledge to fix the problem at hand. If there is a backlash on a social media platform, the digital marketer must have the password or access information ready to hand, and a decision-maker on speed dial regardless of the hour.

Disaster planning tends to take on these new dimensions with digital marketing:

- **Extended hours or staffing** – particularly if rolling out a new product, service or major change to what customers will be receiving (discounts, price hikes and so on).

- **Prior establishment of the tone** – so the digital marketer knows how to speak to customers should public reaction be negative. If the company makes a mistake, the digital response should be forthright, apologetic and solution-oriented. If the brand is now unexpectedly in a bantering-exchange with a celebrity, the digital marketer should have established proper tone and voice in a way that the company can still gain from the exposure but not go too far off message.

- **Security precautions** – these are paramount. If a digital marketer goes on holiday, they must have a backup plan in case something goes awry with customers. And security measures are doubly important when it comes to corporate accounts and presence on social platforms. It seems that every week there is a new example of a company's firewalls being breached or their Twitter or Facebook account being hacked. Do not let that be your company! Establish secure protocols and difficult passwords. Try to reduce the chance a staffer's phone will be forgotten or stolen, with its instant access to your company's social media accounts.

- **Budget limits and budget escalation paths** – if a digital advertising campaign is going better than expected, what is the plan for success? Can you free up budget by appealing to a superior? Planning for success is just as important as being ready for disaster. Digital marketers must be ready to capitalise swiftly on opportunities that present themselves, often in a matter of hours. Jumping into that Instagram battle or taking up a friendly challenge on Twitter may make or break the brand awareness of your company. Even as the digital marketer works to create a seamless, effective brand presence and voice, he or she must be accepting of the idea that there is no such thing as total control.

- **Security measures, death threats or harassment** – in the olden days of traditional marketing, usually only internal company stakeholders or a marketer's immediate boss knew who had created what campaign. But in the digital world of influencer marketing and authentic social media branding, there is more of an emphasis on individual fame and ability to activate your base, so carefully consider how best to respond in the event of harassment or threats.

If you work for a corporation and they have security procedures, become familiar with those. Work to obtain customer support from companies like Twitter, Facebook and Google if you must escalate abusive or negative behaviours on their platforms.

Sadly, the likelihood of this kind of harassment for women is higher than for men, and female digital marketers may need to take extra precautions when out marketing in public and posting on social media channels.

FUTURE-PROOFING YOUR CAREER

Just as medical doctors must keep abreast of the latest scientific studies and medical technologies, so must the digital marketer be vigilant in maintaining their skillset and their creativity on the job. While many digital marketer skills overlap with traditional marketers, there are several that are unique to this field.

Keeping current within your own company

This section is geared toward the digital marketer that has responsibilities to a medium to large-sized company. The digital marketer should understand what the overall business efforts of the company are to better serve them (particularly if these functions are done in different teams or groups outside the organisation). Below is a sampling of the questions a digital marketer should consider to stay current within their company:

- What is the PR strategy for this season and what is the calendar of press outreach?

- What is the (traditional) marketing team's current strategy for this season and what is the calendar of traditional marketing campaigns?

- Are there any opportunities to reduce costs by obtaining discounts of scale on vendors, advertising rates or staffing?

- If your company has employees in the role of product demonstrators or evangelists, are your digital efforts being used to support their presentations, speaking tours, demos and industry events?

- Can your digital marketing efforts support your sales teams, either in promoting the discount or offering they are selling to clients, or by holding online webinars and sales events for clients?

- Does your digital marketing team have regular meetings with customer support to address customer concerns through social media campaigns, or to feed customer complaints gleaned from social media into the formal customer support system?

- Have you channelled insights from your social media campaigns – feedback from customers and requests for new products – back to the company's employees who develop the product?

- If your company employs customer research firms or even has a research and development arm, is the digital marketing team aware of new insights from these internal sources?

- Do you have regular communications pieces, executive-ready, that can inform your company's leadership at once of the efforts you and your team are making via digital channels? Do these pieces have easy to understand graphics and metrics charts to show the wins and losses of each campaign?

Each company will have different communication and collaboration expectations of their marketing professionals. Company culture will need navigation; in a company that already favours open sharing of business division information, a digital marketer should have less difficulty. In a company, un-used to such collaboration, the digital marketer and team may be a grand unifying force that encourages change through sheer practicality. To do a proper job of marketing across multiple platforms, alignment and cross-team understanding must prevail. As each stakeholder sees the development process and sees successful digital marketing results, they will be more inclined to support the next wave of asks and requests for input.

Keeping current through industry events

As social media rose to prominent usage in the United Kingdom and United States, so did a plethora of social media conferences. The names and firms holding these events will change over time, and the keynote speakers may sound impressive, but it can be hard to pick which to attend. How should the digital marketer choose?

First, evaluate what the goals are for attending the conference. Is it to learn more about data analytics and the latest social media tools? That will be a very differently presented conference from one targeted at chief marketing officers (CMOs) and higher-level strategists.

If you are a marketing coordinator or at more of a practical, tactical level, you should look for conferences that have workshops, hands-on-sessions and how-to programming. Sometimes, firms that build digital marketing software will hold conferences (think of Google I/O or Facebook's F8 industry conferences to get the idea). In that case, the digital marketer must weigh the utility of knowing the one platform or software app.

Conference fees can vary widely and travel budgets may be limited, so if the conference has a public livestream you may opt for that rather than attending in person.

Sometimes it is very useful to attend in person as a way of furthering your career and creating contacts with other digital marketers. Learning best practices from other professionals, swapping ideas and gaining insights into industry trends may well happen at morning coffee before the keynote speaker even takes the stage. Get to know conference organisers if you can, so that you can learn more about how they choose speakers and why they accept proposals to speak at their events. For the digital marketer, personal brand is extended by social events in person as well as online. Being there in person offers opportunities to connect with business leaders of companies you might not ordinarily get to talk to about your firm or your own career.

SEO or SEM conferences are a specialised form of marketing conference where SEO or SEM digital marketers gather to talk about best practices and sometimes get search engine representatives to field questions about how to succeed in search engine placement. A few of the best-known conferences of this type are: Search Marketing Expo London,[33] BrightonSEO,[34] International Search Summit,[35] SASCon,[36] SMX[37] and Search Camp.[38] In the United States, the SMX series, organised by searchengineland.com's founder, Danny Sullivan (now at Google), and Mozcon (run by the company formerly known as SEOMoz), are popular. Here, it helps to understand the basic principles of SEO and SEM tactics before attending, to get the most out of the nuanced discussions and debates of the panellists and speakers. Understand that there is always an uneasy tension between the SEO or SEM marketer seeking to achieve organic ranking (without paying), the search engine (who would prefer they get there honestly or pay for search engine ad placement) and a 'black hat' or 'grey hat' set of tactics and firms that use those tactics to play with or game the search engine algorithms for the benefit of their clients and themselves.

Keeping current through online publications and training

As just mentioned, not every digital marketer has the budget or time to attend conferences in other cities. Online courses may be the best way to stay abreast of the latest digital marketing trends. Classes via the online arm of various universities are useful (some are free, some paid), for example:

- http://online.stanford.edu/courses
- https://www.extension.harvard.edu/open-learning-initiative
- http://online-learning.harvard.edu/
- https://www.coursera.org/northwestern
- https://online.wharton.upenn.edu/
- https://www.edx.org/course/digital-marketing-social-media-e-wharton-digitalmarketing1-1x-2
- www.lynda.com
- https://www.udemy.com

Coursera, Udemy, Lynda.com and others can offer the digital marketer innovative ways to think about in their career development. Sites such as Slideshare,[39] a digital repository of presentations, may also serve as a home-grown university. The digital marketer who is hungry to learn more will not find themselves short of materials to read and videos to watch. LinkedIn is also a useful tool – it allows its members to create articles they can share among their professional networks: required reading if you are a digital marketer who wants to connect with others in the field and keep up with the latest thought leadership in your professional circles.

Corporations that create social media management (SMM) tools will often offer informational webinars and events where the digital marketer can familiarise themselves with their tools. For example, the company Sprinklr has an entire section of their website devoted to social media techniques[40] (enabled by their software platform of course). Sprout Social likewise, at the time of writing, offers articles to help bring the digital marketer into their system,[41] as does the American company Hootsuite[42] which broke upon the US social media scene as a Twitter analytics application (it has since expanded into an ecosystem of marketing products).

Publications that discuss social media trends at the time of writing include Mashable,[43] Adweek,[44] TechCrunch,[45] Huffington Post[46] and even non-tech outlets such as CNBC.[47]

In the UK, one can seek training through the Direct Marketing Association (DMA)[48] or learn extra skills through industry reports, such as those offered by the Content Marketing Association (CMA).[49] The IAB is also useful; it represents brands, media owners and agencies in the UK.[50]

The Mobile Marketing Association in the UK encourages the growth of mobile marketing and associated technologies. It delivers thought leadership and information about the UK mobile landscape.[51]

Keeping current by running campaigns and learning from them

Sometimes the best way to future-proof one's digital marketing career is to run a tight ship about metrics and analytics. By constantly challenging assumptions and pushing the understanding of how best to promote their business, digital marketers can still be on the forefront of new technologies and approaches. Careful recordkeeping and insistence on success metrics for every project means that the digital marketer could write white papers and present on the techniques they master. Obviously, businesses hold certain details proprietary, but careful accumulation of social media and digital channel knowledge will continue to propel the digital marketer along his or her career path.

Keeping current by constantly improving soft skills

The greatest strength a digital marketer will have, in the fast-moving business world, is the ability to work with other people – whether it be other departments, a marketing agency supporting the firm, the executive sponsor of the marketing initiative adopting digital channels or a marketing student needing a bit of mentoring and coaching to get his or her first job or internship. Because marketing campaigns are increasingly integrated, and even social media-only campaigns are run on multiple platforms across audiences, careful coordination and clear communication will be evergreen, ever-useful skills to the digital marketer.

Digital marketers are advised to seek out mentors and create support groups for their own careers. Having a cohort of professionals to exchange ideas with and hear about job openings, events and technologies will accelerate the digital marketer's thinking about their work. Kind advice from a mentor about communication styles, how to lead and manage projects, what to do with team dynamics that are not working and other business soft skills will do a lot to push a digital marketer further up the ladder of their profession or organisation.

Keeping current by expanding knowledge of marketing platforms

SEO requires technical knowledge of the underpinnings of a page. CMSs like those running your corporate blog may become outdated or need tweaking to eliminate spam and abuse from the post commentary. Forums and other community support channel software mutate every year. Optimisation of digital campaigns on video-sharing sites requires understanding of the limits of video ad technologies and the nature of broadcasting online. Social media management platforms, where they organise your social media efforts in real time, are continually changing as the target audience shifts from one technology to another. Even understanding the next wave of artificial intelligence (AI), hardware gadgetry and new devices that contribute to an IoT ecosystem will help a digital marketer think of new ways to dazzle their audience.

SUMMARY

The role of the digital marketer, emerging from the need to address audiences reached via digital media and channels, requires a new way of thinking about the marketing role. Instead of approaches that keep the customer at a distance, the digital marketer may be involved in peer-to-peer contact with industry influencers and online communities.

A digital marketing role is one of integration – with other marketers in the firm, with business needs and costs, and with colleagues and stakeholders who need to know how the campaigns are faring. Soft skills and project management acumen serve the digital marketer well, as they figure out how to communicate properly across disciplines in a timely manner.

Not long ago, a traditional marketer had to understand what made good marketing copy and be willing to track success for campaigns that might take days to collate the results. Now, a digital marketing role means working with constant change, continually working to adjust content, and keeping current not only on business trends but technological ones. For digital audiences, popular memes, taste making and backlash to messaging will run at a faster pace than for other marketing audiences. Professional publications, networking and experimentation within campaigns thus play a large part in the digital marketer's success.

3   TOOLS, METHODS AND TECHNIQUES

Consumers have had control of the social landscape since the millennium. Now they can connect to any device – anywhere. PCs, phones, tablets, even smart watches enable them to craft their online personality and communicate their passions. The savvy customer wants to connect with the products that matter to them, right now. They want a personalised experience when they connect and they want it now.

As a digital marketer, it is your job to help them discover products that they will love, connect them with services they need, and help them on their digital journey. You have access to an array of tools, methods and techniques that will enable you to deliver that personalised experience and gain competitive advantage, whilst delivering a new and innovative experience for them.

This chapter gets down to the nuts and bolts of execution for digital marketers, starting with relevant industry standards and professional bodies.

INDUSTRY STANDARDS AND PROFESSIONAL BODIES

Since Dale Carnegie wrote *How to Win Friends and Influence People*[1] in 1936, many marketing ideas have been tried, adopted and adapted to follow the latest trend. The digital marketer would be wise to check out industry standards and seminal pieces of work that will save them from 're-inventing the wheel'.

Skills Framework for the Information Age

Digital marketers working in organisations that use SFIA (Skills Framework for the Information Age[2]) have guidelines about their roles in IT. There are several levels of responsibility for IT professionals, ranging from level 1 – junior members of staff who work under supervision with little autonomy – to level 7 – senior leaders who have significant responsibility for policy, strategy and business.

For example, a digital marketer level 6 will have defined the marketing and planning strategy for their organisation. This will include the integration of digital marketing with traditional marketing methods and will place digital marketing at the centre of all customer communications.

This framework offers good guidance for any company that wants to add structured processes, and roles and responsibilities to their strategy and planning procedures.

Chartered Institute of Marketing

In the UK, the Chartered Institute of Marketing has created a framework of professional marketing competencies which document the knowledge levels and skills required to perform a marketing role.[3]

Marketing Accountability Standards

The Marketing Accountability Standards Board[4] in the US aims to improve the measurement of marketing metrics to enhance the financial performance of a company. It aims to show accountability across the industry and provide guidance and education for marketers.

The American Marketing Association

The American Marketing Association[5] is a community for marketing professionals which commits itself to promoting the highest standard of professional ethical norms and values for its members (practitioners, academics and students). It maintains an up-to-date dictionary of marketing terms.[6]

International Institute of Marketing Professionals

Internationally, the International Institute of Marketing Professionals[7] has created a framework of standard setting processes to develop internationally accepted marketing practices.

Consumer measurement and analytics

US company Nielsen is one of the recognised leaders in measurement and analysis of data. The company began measuring brand advertising analysis in the 1920s, and radio market analysis in the 1930s. It provides statistics on demographics which enable companies to charge more for specific ads that will be shown to specific age demographics.

Nielsen creates its famous TV ratings by collecting information from viewers four times a year. Nielsen's Social Content Ratings measure 'social TV activity across Facebook and Twitter'.[8]

ComScore,[9] another US-based media measurement and analytics company, generates reports on web traffic, video streaming activity and consumer buying power. It installs software on groups of users' machines to analyse online behavioural patterns.

DIGITAL MARKETING-RELATED REGULATIONS

In the UK, the law on advertising is clearly set out by the UK Government which documents how direct marketing, telesales and email marketing should be carried out.[10] Customers must opt in to receive marketing materials such as telephone or email marketing.

Organisations must comply with the General Data Protection Regulation (GDPR) if they are in or do business with the European Union (EU). This aims to give control to internet users who store their data online on servers across the EU. This also specifies how businesses across the EU store customer data, and how users can opt out of marketing communications.

USEFUL TOOLS

There are hundreds of free and commercial social analytics tools available. Many of them do a single task, such as measuring conversions or traffic to a website. Others perform a variety of tasks.

If you want to calculate video views or measure your social media traffic, or see how your social sharing is driving conversions, then you need to do your homework to get the most suitable tool. There are commonalities and techniques that cross most platforms. Tools and measurement technologies will come and go, and digital marketers will need to keep abreast of the latest developments in relevant software. What is important, however, is understanding the frequency, quality and effectiveness of your connection with customers.

Here follows a list of some of the tools that are available to the digital marketer. Some are free, some are commercial. Choose a tool that provides the insights you are looking for. Note that using too many analytics tools can overcomplicate rather than simplify.

Free analytics tools

Some of the tools in the following list have a paid upgrade after a free trial period has elapsed. Others are entirely free.

- **Adpow (http://adpow.com):** Social platform for influencer engagement and reach.

- **Google Analytics (https://www.google.com/analytics):** Digital data and marketing analytics to give a complete picture of the online customer.

- **Google Trends (https://trends.google.com/trends/):** Helpful for digital marketers to see patterns in search trends among Google customers.

- **HubSpot (https://www.hubspot.com):** Inbound marketing traffic analysis and lead conversion toolset.

- **Justmetrics (https://justmetrics.net):** Audience and follower analysis with post-analysis and engagement metrics.

- **Kuku (https://kuku.io):** Social media management syndication platform and analytics to manage multiple social accounts.

- **Quintly (https://www.quintly.com):** Online analytics tool to benchmark and track social media performance against competitors.

- **Similar Web (https://www.similarweb.com):** Analytics tool to monitor the competitions' websites and provide market share analysis.

- **Social Mention (www.socialmention.com):** Analytics tool that displays mentions of your brand, top sources of brand mentions and top users mentioning the brand name or term.

- **Sprout Social (https://sproutsocial.com):** Social media management, advocacy and analytics software.

- **SumAll (https://sumall.com):** Social media and metrics tracker and analytics platform.

- **Weelytics (https://weelytics.com):** Weelytics tracks website visitors, interactions and metrics, publishing to analytics tools such as Google Analytics.

- **Wishpond (https://www.wishpond.com):** Wishpond enables marketers to create landing pages and manage customer leads.

Commercial analytics tools

These are tools that must be paid for.

- **Birdsong Analytics (www.birdsonganalytics.com):** Pay-as-you-go social media reports for Twitter, Instagram, YouTube and Facebook.

- **Brand 24 (https://brand24.com):** Brand mention analytics with influence score and sentiment analysis.

- **Brandwatch (https://www.brandwatch.com):** Social listening and reputation management platform across blogs, forums, videos, reviews, images, Twitter and Facebook.

- **Crowdbabble (https://www.crowdbabble.com):** Analytics platform for Facebook, Instagram, Twitter, LinkedIn and Snapchat. Also analyses hashtags and competitors.

- **GetSocial (https://getsocial.io):** GetSocial tracks sharing not easily recognised by social sharing, including private shares across Facebook, Twitter, WhatsApp and email.

- **Lithium (https://www.lithium.com):** Social media analytics platform that uses six 'health factors' to create an index-like credit score to analyse the health of your online community.

- **Open Influence (https://openinfluence.com):** Marketing platform to create branded content for identified influencers.

- **Sotrender (https://www.sotrender.com):** Social analytics for Facebook, Twitter, Instagram and YouTube analysing top posts, competitor comparison and audience analytics.

- **Synthesio (www.synthesio.com):** Social media intelligence platform that measures and delivers key performance indicators (KPIs) and ROI metrics.

- **Visibrain (www.visibrain.com/en/):** A media monitoring platform for marketers, monitoring brands, influencers and trends.

Content creation tools

There are many content creation tools to help you publish the best content for your company. Some help with research, some with spell checking, grammar and formatting. Some are useful to help with SEO. Here are a few tools to help you with your marketing tasks.

- **Audacity (www.audacityteam.org/):** A free open source downloadable tool to enable you to record and edit audio content across multiple tracks.

- **Canva (https://www.canva.com):** A free tool providing templates and images for the creation of custom collages, flyers and titled images.

- **Designspiration (https://www.designspiration.net):** A free image search service which displays relevant images after a search. Some of these images are subject to copyright so correct permission must be obtained for use.

- **Kapost (https://kapost.com):** A paid-for tool that enables targeted content to be sent to the correct set of customers and organised to match the creative brief.

- **Picmonkey (https://www.picmonkey.com):** A commercial tool (after a free trial) which enables you to edit, manipulate and store custom images and collages.

- **Pictaculous (http://pictaculous.com/):** A free tool that helps you to use the correct colour palette that will suit an image on the web.

- **Piktochart (https://piktochart.com/):** A free tool (with commercial options) which enables you to create graphics from a library of images, templates and fonts.

- **QuotesCover (http://quotescover.com):** A free tool that enables you to overlay your own quote or choose from a library of attributed quotes and overlay them on to an image.
- **Ubersuggest (https://ubersuggest.io/):** This free tool suggests new keywords for your content that you might not have considered to help your content climb through page rank results.
- **Unsplash (https://unsplash.com):** A free set of images for use in online content.

FRAMEWORKS AND METHODOLOGIES

Digital marketing requires rapid response to marketplace changes, but there are frameworks and methodologies that can save time and help you to organise and structure day-to-day work. Knowing your level of competency as a digital marketer within these professional best practices and evaluation frameworks can also orient you properly in your career progression.

The company's digital marketing playbook

The term 'playbook' might not be as familiar to workers in the UK, but in the US the term is well known. The word comes from the world of sport, where a notebook containing descriptions and diagrams of the 'plays' of American football teams are used as a set of tactics to gain competitive advantage. As in sports events, real-time marketplace conditions can change minute to minute, so being able to refer to assets and tactics for using them in a handy reference document can mean the difference between campaign disaster and campaign recovery.

To capture a structured, strategic approach to online marketing, a guidance document – the playbook – is necessary so that all marketers in the company are aware of the digital marketing goals and how to use the correct strategies and tactics to achieve the marketing objectives for the target audience.

This enables digital marketers to follow these structured frameworks to plan and execute the marketing plan, discover where they need to start their campaign to achieve the best results, and learn from best practices.

Ideally, a playbook is contained in a wiki or other centralised repository that can be updated as marketplace changes occur or as digital marketing ability grows across the company. The devil is in the detail, so to speak.

High-level goals for the digital marketing playbook should be:

- To clearly detail strategy and planning guidance for marketing campaigns.
- To provide industry-specific best practices for digital marketers.
- To provide a comprehensive framework for delivery of marketing campaigns and strategies.
- To provide frameworks for measurement and optimisation of campaigns.
- To detail disaster planning information and an effective recovery plan, should the worst happen.

Digital marketing is a rapidly evolving media, so strategic planning guidance can equip teams with the knowledge to prepare for new social platforms when planning campaigns.

The strategy in a digital marketing playbook should define how the business relationship with customers will change, what resources are needed to effect this change and what blockers, if any, there are to making this happen.

The playbook will contain relevant metrics and have well-defined objectives that will be the foundation for the entire social media strategy and KPIs. Customer service goals, research and development metrics or projected audience reach should be included, as should campaign execution strategies.

Each individual campaign or campaign type will have metrics specific to that effort, useful in understanding when measures described in the playbook should be taken. (For example, 'If the cost per conversion rises above X amount, we have a standing policy to pull the campaign and wait for better auction conditions.')

Leveraging the playbook

The playbook should be a living document or set of resources that are continually updated as each campaign moves forward. It should provide a record of past successes so that future teams can build upon campaign achievements, mitigate issues and carry out disaster planning if an issue arises. As the audience evolves, the playbook can be used as a resource to better find and engage with the audience, groups or individuals that the company is not connected to. Planning audits – such as for SEO or social platforms – can use the playbook to show scorecard metrics and goals and carry out campaign optimisation.

As campaigns are completed, activities that did not deliver the expected results can be documented and refined for future campaigns. Social media is continually evolving; therefore, the digital marketer needs to be able to make a long-term commitment to ensure that any digital campaign is aligned against the playbook goals. The playbook structure should be flexible enough to be refined as new platforms appear that will be of use to the digital marketer and updated whenever the company policies or scorecards change.

Campaign planning

Goals need to be set for every marketing campaign. These goals need to be fixed, with objectives specified, and the correct channels identified. This could include several streams of activities, some running concurrently. The overall campaign plan could be broken down into several phases, or milestones, have different objectives for different audience segments and detail differing resources needed throughout the campaigns.

Go-To-Market document

Once the audience has been defined, the objective has been stated and the expected outcome has been documented, a digital marketer needs to create a Go-To-Market (GTM) document, detailing the strategy and choice of tools for the campaign. Each GTM document follows the overarching principles and methods defined in the company playbook and details how each campaign will be executed.

This document – which could form the basis for a team strategy discussion – could contain the following questions:

1. How will your strategy change your relationship with your customers in the short, medium or long term?
2. What resources (people, tools, budget) do you need to carry out your plan?
3. How will the new plan affect new behaviours and change relationships with your customers?
4. What dependencies does your strategy have? How can you ensure that these dependencies are available when needed?
5. How will you support this plan over time?
6. How will you scale the plan if it becomes successful? Can you replicate it?
7. What internal or external blockers do you need to overcome in order to achieve success?
8. What tactics, tools or technologies will you use for your plan? Document why you have chosen these tools or technologies.
9. What are the most important features required of each tactic or tool?
10. What new skills or training do you or your team members need in order to succeed?

11. What resources and processes will you need to mitigate these risks?

12. What are the associated costs? Document whether these costs are fixed costs or ongoing.

13. Do you need to engage an external vendor or partner to execute the plan? Document the specific actions the external person or team will need to carry out.

14. What could go wrong with this plan? Document potential risks.

15. How can you minimise these risks and minimise a potential crisis?

Defining who – The audience

Marketers need to define and segment their audience so that a marketing campaign can be as effective as possible. They need to identify where the audience already engages online and how they prefer to communicate. Building a good relationship with the audience will depend on how they already interact with the technologies they choose. They might be online 'lurkers', interacting little but watching everything that you post. They may be 'likers', randomly liking posts and statuses to show that they have seen them. Or, they may be 'lovers', who are fans of the brand, love everything the brand does and are eager to broadcast brand messages to their network. The goal of the marketer is to give the lurkers information to keep them happy, post enough interesting and engaging content to encourage the likers, and develop a suitable influencer programme to reward and encourage the lovers of the brand.

Marketers need to create personas for the types of people they will target. Personas attempt to ensure that all types of behaviour are considered. Not everyone has the same shopping habits as you do, so marketing to one type of customer will not appeal to others with a different approach to purchasing.

Digital marketers need to analyse how their audience interacts online to determine the best way to connect with them. They also need to find a way to identify influencers in their audience who will spread their message for them. Most importantly, the audience the marketer intends to attract should be at the centre of the marketing campaign.

Defining why – Business marketing objectives

Understanding the audience is vital to the success of an online campaign, but the campaign must be carefully crafted too. Marketers should align their campaigns to the overall goals of the business. They should ensure that their campaign will deliver the right expected business outcome, and generate leads, interaction or sales. A clear objective should make it easier to establish achievement of that objective.

That objective might be something as simple as getting a conversation going with some targeted customers in advance of a new product launch. It might be to generate influencers to spread the word about your brand or it might be a simple listening programme to enable the company to understand how their customers feel about them and using that feedback to improve the product. Whether your business objectives are creating awareness or recruiting talent, your objectives need to be clearly defined and aligned to your marketing strategy.

Defining how – The joined-up approach

A good marketing campaign spans different online channels and optimises as the campaign progresses. The channels could encompass traditional channels such as TV and radio, online channels such as video or blogs and embed a social element, such as a hashtag or search term, that the audience could use. Ensuring success means bringing channels as disparate as blogs, video and print together in a coherent campaign across paid, owned and earned marketing channels.

Having a constant monitoring and measurement framework is paramount to justifying a return on your marketing investment (ROMI), but it is also useful to gauge the pulse of a campaign. Users will very quickly voice their opinions if a campaign is going poorly. Listening – and responding quickly – will ensure that the campaign is as successful as possible.

There is more on the use of different channels and the importance of having a consistent message across them in the next section.

> The digital marketing playbook should go into detail on how you plan to carry out the strategy. You will need a set of frameworks, methodologies and worksheets to organise your tactical approach, document your listening plan (how you will gain customer insights to inform the campaign) and deliver your execution plan.

Defining what – Choosing the correct tool

In all campaigns, marketers must note that there is not one prescribed formula for success. As digital technologies and social platforms evolve, so must the marketing campaign. Whether that is through chatbot technology, AI, voice-enabled devices or robots, the campaign must be adjusted to best engage the customer.

It is often of benefit to tabulate an overview of strategies and themes by intended audience type such as in Table 3.1, which shows strategies for a furniture company's line of modular furniture.

Table 3.1 Overview of strategies by audience type

Customer type	Strategy	Campaign
Managers, generalists and manufacturing brand specialists	Educate and inform whilst uncovering new opportunities and extending reach	**Always on modules campaign (Q3)** GTM campaign for modular classic furniture

(Continued)

Table 3.1 (Continued)

Customer type	Strategy	Campaign
Consumers and savvy shoppers	Drive app adoption for modular furniture AR app	**AR is everywhere campaign (Q4)** In conjunction with Real Homes show campaign
Furniture store owners and partners	Uncover new oportunities for upsell of modular office furniture	**Mobile worker campaign (Q2)** Showing how the Internet of Things is enabling the third space amongst millennials who use coffee shops and shared spaces to work
University faculties	Increase student retention and attendance	**Savvy workspaces campaign (Q3/4)** Offering modular study areas with quiet zones and always on infrastructure

Multi-channel consistency

It is important for a brand to have a consistent message. If a campaign is going to be delivered across a variety of channels, it is important that the message resonates offline and online across all of them.

Customers want to connect with the brand on the channel they prefer.

Customers view the brand as an entity – whether they are in a shop, viewing an online store or interacting with the brand on social media channels. Consistency across all different channels – online and offline – is vital to multi-channel success. A holistic view needs to be taken of all your outbound and inbound channels.

If a television advertisement stresses one message, the company's email newsletter and Facebook page ought to reinforce that message. If the goal is to increase Twitter support and engagement for a brand, other media put out by the company across different channels must have the same hashtag across platforms so that someone seeing the materials can join the conversation. This helps in identifying which channel is performing the best.

Whether a marketing message is on a website, an email received on a customer's mobile device, an online video or a leaflet through the door, that message needs to be crafted to encourage the best response from the medium. Programmatic advertising will ensure success and memory retention in customers. A good messaging strategy will encourage customers to buy – regardless of the channel.

Customers will often browse shops, then go home and buy the product online. They might see a product on one channel and decide to purchase on another channel. If a marketer can follow those changes, such as offline to online, TV to mobile or offline to mobile, with a consistent campaign, then they will see an increase in sales. The customer wants to choose which channel to communicate on during most stages of their customer journey. Marketers need to make sure that they connect with the customer when they are ready to engage with the brand.

Unfortunately, not every marketer delivers campaigns across multiple channels, nor offers consistency across those channels. Budget cuts often mean that the marketing team must 'do more with less'. Delivering the correct message to the correct audience is important but getting them ready to act on that message is vital. Delivering that message across different channels increases customer spend by three to four times according to the SAS Institute.[11]

> Customer behaviour changes depending on the time of day. Buying patterns may change from computer and TV, to mobile device and TV during the evening when the main PC has been shut down for the evening. Weekends too will see a change in behaviour.

Customers that see ads across screens such as computers, smartphones and tablets in addition to TV have much greater recall of the content of the ad and feel more positive opinions about the advertised object.[12] Advertising on second, third or even fourth screens have better responses.

But which channels should the marketer choose? The vast number of channels available gives the consumer a lot of choice and control over the buying process. Certain channels go well together and deliver high results. According to a Media Daily News analysis there are seven pairs of media devices and channels that go particularly well together.[13]

1. computer and mobile device;
2. mobile device and TV;
3. computer and TV;
4. mobile device and radio;
5. computer and radio;
6. radio and TV;
7. print and TV.

The challenge for brands that wish to use this approach is the number of channels that need to be managed. More channels mean that more effort, time and money are needed to make sure that campaigns get the expected outcome. Customer queries and comments need to be addressed and sales leads followed through. All your chosen channels should work seamlessly together.

Multi-channel marketing is not always a cut and dried success. It needs to be done correctly. A digital marketer's campaign needs to be completely integrated and planned correctly across all their intended channels. Each channel must have a relevant message that will convince the customer that the brand is one to be trusted. If the messaging has not been targeted correctly then it will be ineffective and the audience will not respond as you hope.

The successful multi-channel campaign should be measured against segments of your audience that do not see the multi-channel ad. Setting up control groups in this way will enable the marketer to ascertain which media has the most take-up and works the best for the business. Adding data to the marketing mix will enable further campaigns to be more successful. The successful marketer should know what touchpoint triggered an effective response.

So how does the digital marketer make sure that multi-channel marketing efforts will be successful? Aside from consistency, making sure that you have one view of the customer data across all channels is more than collecting data. Try to understand the customer. Use data analytics to predict what the customer will do across the customer life cycle and optimise the campaign if a negative trigger happens.

Create a workflow for event triggers. This could be an email if the customer fails to complete a purchase or a chatbot popping up for assistance if the customer spends too much time on one landing page before the sale. Make sure that the trigger events work across different segments of the audience. If a trigger does not work, then create another workflow process.

Triggers such as attribution modelling can be used to mark stages in the sales pipeline that have been successful in attributing to the sale. If the customer proceeds to click through to a sale, then the model is considered to have been 100 per cent successful. Other milestones or touchpoints throughout the customer journey can also be measured.

Although multi-channel marketing is complex, it is the best way for the marketer to connect with the customer.

Customer engagement

For marketers to understand how their audience will respond to their marketing efforts, they try to gain an insight into what motivates and excites their audience. They then need to plan how to connect with their audience, how often they should communicate with them, how to address their concerns and how to capture details of the engagement. This process of understanding usually goes through several steps.

Utilising the playbook

A company needs to be relevant to its audience in order to ensure success with any digital marketing campaign.

A digital marketing playbook should define strategy, which should help to ensure that the scenarios a marketer proposes, and the procedures documented in the playbook, align campaigns and offers with the audience.

The different segments of an audience might need different execution plans, documented in the playbook, to ensure that the marketing campaign is effective at the chief information officer (CIO) level and the consumer level. For instance, a campaign could embrace the academic sector, sharing stories about students, and encouraging innovation. It could target the B2B market, sharing partner stories and producing collateral that can be shared. The plan could simply be to find and engage influencers and micro-influencers to increase the volume and conversation about the product.

Identifying the right channel to get the best reach

Digital marketing allows you to craft a story and amplify it across different forms of media to connect with your breadth audience and forge deeper relationships with your depth audience.

Leveraging the right channel is a key part of your marketing plan. Consumers see a huge array of information each day across a plethora of channels, so the marketer must consider which channel will be best for the campaign.

Primarily, the marketer needs to:

- Identify the people that are to receive the marketing communications. These will be the people that will either buy the product or respond to the communication in the desired way.

- Carry out research to see which channels they use to receive information. Short or simple messages might be most effective across a social media channel; long or complex communications may require the use of a different channel.

- Calculate the cost of communicating this message across each channel. Channels such as TV will be expensive, and some publishers will charge more than others. Social channels are little or no cost, depending on whether you pay for promoted posts or not.

The marketer needs to consider not only connecting with the enthusiast, but also with the sceptical, negative or critical customer. To this tricky group, digital marketers should try to improve perception of the company and its brand(s).

- Define what response is needed from this communication. Do you want to engage or surface influencers, or assess customer satisfaction for the product? Make sure all comments are responded to in accordance with your defined framework.

- Create a list of all suitable channels and compare the performance of each channel. Make sure that each channel has a set of services such as customer relationship management, order management, product management and issue management. If these are standardised, then any fresh marketing channel that comes online can quickly be utilised.

> It is important to recognise the differing amounts of effort needed to produce content on different channels. Whilst it is easy to take a picture and upload it on social sites, full production videos with voiceovers take considerable effort and should be built into the plan.

Listen

The successful marketer will need to fully understand their audience and how they work. They should know their media habits, which device they prefer to use – and when – and adjust their marketing to suit. Digital marketers need to anticipate changes in the online landscape and adjust resources to suit new media.

Real-time listening gives instant insight on how a campaign plan is progressing and will highlight areas to improve. It can be useful to carry out a listening audit which should take about four weeks. This involves capturing data on how often the audience uses a tool or channel, the level of conversation and interaction on each channel and the tone and voice of the conversation for each channel. The listening audit can either be carried out manually by a member of the marketing team, or an analytics tool can be used to capture this data.

The audit will enable the digital marketer to make sure that the chosen channels in the plan are the same channels the audience uses. It takes this amount of time for a good dataset to be collected. The listening plan should feed into the planning strategy and a social media strategy. It enables the marketer to make sure that the plan is working well. It will also surface any areas that need to be addressed to help users more effectively. Listening will also surface influencers who are talking about the brand, as well as brand fan sites, engaged communities and brand evangelists. Once the audit has been carried out, then the marketing team can create a benchmark for performance against each platform for the campaign. This benchmarking will provide relevant KPIs for the campaign and should match objectives.

Build

After the foundation for a successful engagement strategy is laid, the build phase begins. The build phase of a campaign could be as simple as creating a content calendar, developing training for the team or designing a creative brief for the agency. It also could be significantly more complex, such as developing a new media platform to capture Vox pops (the voice of the public, used to capture opinions) or the pulse of the audience right now. Whatever the build phase contains, it is important that it ties in with the digital strategy for customer engagement and overall business strategy.

The metrics dashboard should be created during the build phase, mapping the KPIs to metrics. This could be a simple spreadsheet – to give an all-up view of the campaign progress and show adjustments that are made to the ongoing campaign. Engagement metrics should be determined beforehand, and success levels established.

Whilst a content calendar is easy to create, it often forms the core of all marketing activity. It might contain details on how many social media posts to create or when to write a particular blog post. However, in a multi-channel campaign, these activities need to be synchronised with activities such as a TV or radio campaign, or a new product launch. Content calendars need to document buzz generation activities that start months before the go-live date or event. The marketer will need to manage the differing types of content that go on each channel, and when these should best be posted to engage customers.

Engage

Customer engagement does not often run as the marketer predicts. Customers vary in their online actions and, despite the level of unpredictability, the marketer must prepare how to respond when dealing with enquiries, information, complaints, dissatisfaction and anger. Each style of inbound comment, when discovered, must be assessed for its tone and manner, considered and responded to. The customer engagement framework therefore must take these situations into account as much as possible.

Detractors are across all social media and will take every opportunity to talk about a product or brand in a negative way. Their comments may be inflammatory, misleading, baiting or obscene. An organisation's digital marketing playbook should state what needs to be done when detractors, critics and flamers continue to attack the brand. If they continue to harass, it's important that there is an escalation plan in place, so key people such as customer support, team vendor budget owners, executive stakeholders and PR teams are made aware of the problem and can help the digital marketer draft an appropriate response.

An example of an engagement framework is shown in Figure 3.1.

Figure 3.1 Online engagement considerations

Different channels require different amounts of effort and elicit different results. A wiki might be easy to write – but do not set your expectations too high if you want engagement. Blog writing will take more effort – it needs to be well written, interesting and engaging – yet the results should make the effort worthwhile.

Online forums are useful across industries – especially if the forum offers help. They are 'evergreen'; posts can be discovered through search engines months after first publication and provide a useful pointer to the brand. On the other hand, ephemeral tools such as Snapchat, Weibo and Twitter are good for an instant signpost to a resource – however, they cannot easily be discovered and, unless embedded in a blog post or article, are lost to searchers.

Above all, your engagement strategy needs to be workable for your brand. Your primary goal is to encourage conversation. Make certain that the brand is listening to its users and responding promptly with the appropriate tone and voice.

Monitor

Often marketers focus on easily accessible metrics for customer engagement, such as followers, likes and shares. These metrics, whilst useful, are not actually as important as other quantitative and qualitative metrics.

Quantitative metrics describe volumes such as the volume of the audience talking about your products or the reach gained by a campaign. Qualitative metrics describe emotional qualities, such as how strongly do customers feel about the new branding, how energised are the interactions and how influential are the people giving those opinions?

It is also important to track the metrics that show that the campaign has been successful. Whatever that metric is, make sure that each set metric matches the original defined objectives.

If you want to understand what people think of your brand, a key objective is listening. Monitoring will not only tell you how many people are talking about your brand (quantitative) but how they feel about the brand (qualitative – sentiment).

If you are creating an influencer programme, the objective is engagement. The quantitative metric is measuring how many enthusiastic ambassadors are broadcasting brand messages; the qualitative metric is the sentiment in their messages and the quality of their discussions.

Monitoring success is easy – but getting the correct measurements that mean something is much harder than you think. Creating your all-up marketing campaign will take considerable time and resources. Maintaining, monitoring and optimising the campaign will take even more time. Make sure you plan for this.

Managing a potential crisis

Having an effective and workable plan in place will help to mitigate any issues if a crisis occurs. After all, the difference between a crisis and an emergency is that everyone is drilled in emergency procedures (think fire crews and cabin crew). With an effective crisis management framework, you can add your social media emergency drill to your standard implementation plan, drill everyone and make everyone aware of what they need to do when – or if – the crisis happens.

This framework and its relationship to the playbook document will need to be revised as conditions change and best practices alter.

Everyone in the company needs to be aware of what to do if a crisis occurs. Offer training sessions or elearning for the business and new members of staff joining after the initial training has been completed. Although everyone in the business will not be using social media in their day job, they need to be aware of the impact that it might have on the business and they should become brand advocates offline.

Outbound communications must be done with the knowledge of line managers and human resources (HR), using a recognised spokesperson trained to talk to the media. Make sure all channels are monitored.

If ongoing communications need to change because of the way that the audience perceives the current marketing, then this should be done rapidly, ensuring that everyone has been fully briefed on the new plan. This could be the cessation of marketing activities if a social media crisis is detrimental to future marketing activities.

In Figure 3.2 is a simplified set of actions to consider in mitigating an online crisis.

Figure 3.2 Crisis management considerations

Storytelling

A great marketing campaign takes the customer on a journey, inspiring them and motivating them. Creating content to keep your customers engaged requires good storytelling ability. Humans naturally tell stories to their friends and colleagues. It helps us to communicate more effectively and get our point across.

Effective marketers create stories that help customers understand the product and build empathy with any characters. Stories must have a clear end, or outcome, and a positive resolution. The message must stick in the minds of the reader, or viewer, and change their perception about the brand.

There are different storytelling techniques to help you get your message across.[14] Nested loop stories help the marketer to position the brand vision along with the campaign, while sparklines help the marketer portray a vision of how the users' world will be improved with the new product adoption.

Nested loops: The telling of the peripheral story detailing how you reached a decision for example, or how you approached a challenge by doing something in a completely new way to solve the overriding problem.

Sparklines: These distinguish between life in an ideal world and the reality of the situation. They allow you to compare and contrast reality and aspiration.

A good story should transcend the media it is originally created for. It should underpin the whole marketing message. People are moved by stories delivered over different media by audio, video and written content. Digital marketers should share their stories in a way that will align best with customer needs.

Handling creative agencies

Larger corporations may have established policies and procedures for working with marketing or creative agency vendors, often dictated by the procurement department. In that case, the digital marketer should follow the company process to the letter, taking care to document and keep communication constant.

The bidding process

Often a company will have policies around how vendors may bid for company work. The list below is a generic example of how the process may work for business enterprises seeking creative or marketing help.

- Often creative marketing agencies respond to a request for proposal (RFP), where the digital marketer for a company lays out the goals and objectives and preferred channels for a campaign, and has multiple agencies come up with formatted proposals for how they would do the campaign. Ideally, requirements within an RFP are detailed enough and the winning proposal is detailed enough that it is not too hard to create a mutually agreeable statement of work based on it.

- Often the SOW forms the basis for a formal contract between company and vendor, and the SOW serves to protect both the creative agency and the company paying for the work. With everything spelled out, neither side can complain they did not know what was being agreed upon. A SOW may be based on a company template, or the digital marketer will have to sit with the agency and help them to generate one. It is essential to work through any gaps from the RFP that would end up in the contract between the agency and the digital marketer's company.

- In larger corporations with 'preferred vendors', prior legal agreements between the corporation and vendor govern the statement of work, invoicing and payments. If you find that your company does not have that infrastructure in place, proceed carefully with the legal department and make all work expectations and deliverables on both sides as clear as possible.

- A contract between the company and agency – written by lawyers or (US) attorneys – comes at the end of the work discussions and the details of what the agency will provide, and what the company will provide, are cleared up. At this point, together you have ironed out with the agency what the work is, who will do it, when it will be done and how much you think the agency should be paid (and when they will be paid).

The agency relationship: Money, time and expectations

Prior to hiring an agency, the digital marketer or their team must be clear on how much budget they have for this purpose, and try to structure the campaign to come under the budget in case of problems or unexpected cost overruns. Ideally, your contract is scoped so that if there are cost overruns, you have not overspent your true budget limit. Other considerations are:

- All non-disclosure agreements must be signed before work begins – and sometimes even earlier than that, depending on the sensitivity of the campaign. Playbooks, brand and style guidelines are the property of the corporation, not the hired agency, and it's often expected that they are kept completely confidential.

- Payment schedules should coincide with when deliverables are approved and turned in by the agency – usually not before work is complete. The digital marketer should check with finance or legal departments in their company for advice.

- If executive approvals within the digital marketer's company take a long time or will be slowed by a person being on holiday, the digital marketer should budget that time into the calendar for the campaign and alert the agency ahead of time about how much time the review process will require.

- Both the digital marketer and the agency need to set up recurring meetings and checkpoints, in order to ensure the work stays on the right track and the agency is rewarded for hitting key milestones. If there are periods during the campaign when unusual amounts of coverage are expected (say for the launch of a product on social media or a time when assets need to be coordinated with other marketing outputs) both sides need to have that in their project timeline.

117

- Key points of contact on both sides need to be established and, if needed, off-business-hours contact information should be swapped. There should always be someone available on both sides to make a decision on an issue so that the project continues to move forward.

- Status reports on progress and metrics for the success of campaigns should be reported in a timely fashion from the agency to the digital marketer. Especially if the digital marketer is paying for dashboards or other metrics rollups – ensure all accesses have been created for review ahead of time. You do not want to get to the end of a contract and realise that the agency erroneously reported on the wrong metrics.

- Though agency employees are working on contract, it pays to be as civil and courteous to them as possible. It is always possible for the digital marketer to learn from the agency being hired, and often people career-switch between in-house marketing and agency work.

Working for an agency can give you a broad range of résumé-building experiences, but it often involves long hours and high pressure. On the other hand, working inside one company allows you to dive deeply into that company's marketing processes, though possibly still with long hours and high pressure (depending on the company).

- Sometimes, a campaign is so innovative the agency may want to enter it for an industry award competition. A digital marketer should make sure the agency informs them and gets their permission on this use of their collateral. They should also ensure that the PR department knows of the entry, in case a win can help them in securing positive news coverage for the marketer's company.

Organisational communication

It is important for companies to ensure that relevant communication flows towards and between the correct teams in a company. Both company-wide messages and team-to-team messages should ensure that everyone involved is fully aware of their roles and responsibilities during the campaign, and that key stages are communicated to the right people to complete the task effectively.

Project management skills and related tools

Software tools will simplify the execution of a campaign and ensure that everyone involved in the campaign has the most up-to-date information about the campaign.

- Tools such as Microsoft Excel, Google Sheets, Microsoft Project, Atlassian's JIRA and Trello are useful for project tracking. What software is used doesn't matter as long as the format clearly communicates what is happening and what has been agreed upon for what deadlines.

- Shared calendar and timeline software tools such as Google Calendar, Microsoft Outlook and IBM Connections will help the digital marketer and their campaign team to have a constant shared understanding of what is happening when, and what the countdown tasks will be until the campaign goes live.

- Any project documentation gets stale rapidly – digital marketers will need Slack, HipChat, Skype or other chat client tools as well as email to stay connected with teammates.

It's important that digital marketers always plan buffer time into projects as they use these project management tools – agencies or other dependencies may make the campaign creation take longer than expected. These windows of time may be used for stakeholder review, validation and testing of message or platform setup.

If resources are available, a digital marketer can plan pilot or message testing and usability testing into the project with enough time to modify creatively if the tests show people don't like the campaign or product. This is important in an agency's client work to ensure the client likes the direction before committing all the resources.

If working with a creative agency, they have likely already solved this problem and picked the appropriate software tools or storage combination to allow customers to review the initial creative work, videos and prototype websites. Dropbox, Hightail (formerly YouSendIt), Google Drive, Microsoft's OneDrive and other online sharing services that ensure file privacy and security are appropriate here. Video sharing platforms such as Vimeo and YouTube can often create restricted access points where a customer can view in-progress videos.

Communicating with stakeholders

Stakeholders, especially those responsible for the digital marketing budget, will expect updates on a regular basis. Since it would be unwieldy to have those people physically present and commenting in every team meeting, it's important to have documentation and meeting cadence that filters only what they need to know.

Some stakeholders may be remote or travelling, so accessible documentation and communication they can check asynchronously is useful.

A digital marketer may plan on touching base with execs prior to launch (results of pilot and testing are good to present here) and during and after campaigns so they can see how they went.

Post-mortem and reflection meeting

This is the process by which, after the campaign, what worked and what did not work is discussed among team members in a constructive atmosphere. Learning points are recorded. New processes are derived or old ones are changed to work more effectively or nimbly.

Meetings should be concise and everyone attending the meeting should be given the opportunity to deliver a succinct report about the campaign. The chair of the meeting should take steps to ensure that the meeting does not stray off topic or become antagonistic as blame is apportioned. They should also ensure that all relevant points are covered and an effective set of actions are defined for the next campaign.

Technology-assisted marketing

Technology has unleashed potential for large and small businesses. Freed from traditional media, marketing campaigns can become integrated, innovative and interactive. Marketers can take their customers on a journey across different media. Customers can stay in touch with the brand wherever and whenever they want to, from whatever device they choose to use.

Voice activated AI devices such as Amazon Echo or Google Home have already been used in marketing campaigns. In 2017, these smart home assistants responded to TV ads aired in the US.[15] The spoken request activated the devices to search for information on the web. Initially these devices responded to a Super Bowl ad, prompting Burger King to air a similar ad to trigger devices.

Visual marketing, especially live video, will continue to grow and come to dominate the marketing landscape as mobile bandwidth penetration such as 4G and 5G expands its coverage. Image-driven platforms will continue to dominate the landscape as their popularity grows. Bots will become pervasive across customer service, workflow and campaign management.

Virtual reality is gaining in popularity, and ripe for the digital marketer to take advantage of in carefully crafted campaigns. Instant stories that disappear after a set amount of time online are perfect for buzz generation, creating a 'must have' attitude amongst customers.

The opportunities for the digital marketer are almost endless. The smart digital marketer will use all new and emerging tools at their disposal to create a compelling message that increases customer base and improves sales targets.

SUCCESSES AND FAILURES

Each company and each campaign presents different goals and different metrics by which to evaluate success, and of course every channel or platform requires analysis.

Keeping to industry standard practices of measurement help to make the evaluation of success or failure consistent across campaigns and enable the tracking of month over month or year over year trends as well. As mentioned previously, setting up success metrics and goals before embarking on campaigns also helps in later evaluation, if only to provide a plan from which to deviate.

As public sentiment evolves over time, and public attention shifts and moves rapidly, it's possible for a campaign to begin well and end poorly, or do well globally but fail locally. While digital marketers try to instrument platforms and content well enough to understand the impact of campaigns, they are working against the fluidity of public discourse and news events of the day. What might have been a successful launch under other circumstances can get derailed by a national victory or disaster, with big breaking news drowning out any kind of commercial message. So even as the digital marketer strives for absolutes – wins and percentage points – he or she should remember that social campaigns are complex and may give unusual or mixed results.

Generally, digital marketing **success metrics** fall under the following:

- Did the customer see or become exposed to the marketing content successfully?
- Did the customer click, swipe, save, share or otherwise engage with the marketing content?
- Upon seeing the digital content, was the customer guided or driven to purchase?
- Upon seeing the digital content, did the customer 'buy in to the brand' – join a loyalty programme, sign on for a newsletter, follow on a social media channel?
- Is the customer amplifying brand messages or brand perception on social channels?
- Has the customer converted to an influencer – that is, has he or she become an advocate for the company, brand or product, and has a larger than normal following?

Digital marketing **failure markers** may include the following:

- Did the campaign fall short of expected reach (by content quality failure, exposure difficulties or any other condition)?
- Once exposed, did the customers react according to projected forecast for engagement (or industry standard) or did they fail to engage with the content or campaign?
- Did the content appear 'tone deaf' or fail to take into account market or sociological forces at play in the public arena? Was it easy to take the content the wrong way, and did people do so?
- Did the customer complete the conversion 'funnel' at rates lower than expected for that channel, medium or ad platform?
- Did the campaign result in the baseline level of expected sales?

- If seeking brand awareness or loyalty, did the customer reject the brand's overtures? Unsubscribe from the newsletter or service? Reject the brand's projection of itself as invalid or untrue?

- Has the campaign succeeded in raising brand awareness but not moved the needle on areas the company finds more important (sales, conversions, signups)?

- Was the campaign too successful in its giveaways, promos or discounts, so that when normal conversation or outreach occurs, the customers are now only trained to look for the freebies?

- Have customers or influencers turned against the product or brand, fostering awareness of the campaign or company as something consumers should avoid?

Occasionally, a campaign will generate success or failure in areas that the campaign did not intend or was not set to measure. These situations present the greatest opportunities for learning for the digital marketer. For that reason, it may be good to set up success metrics for a campaign that are standard across the digital marketer's campaigns, regardless of intent, so that unexpected effects are caught and measured.

The following examples are a mix of successes, failures and in-between results that digital marketers may use in thinking about their own goals and campaigns.

Success frameworks

Different digital marketing agencies will provide their own frameworks for clients, and in-house digital marketers will be following company policies around measurement, budget and success. For this reason, it is difficult to craft a one-size-fits-all success framework – particularly when technical advances or changes in public sentiment can render once-viable approaches useless. The digital marketer needs to be nimble and work with their team to evolve what will work for their business at the present moment in time.

After each campaign, digital marketers should hold post-mortem meetings or retrospectives with their team and determine what the learning points were this time around. Aside from the specific campaign markers listed above, the overall success of digital marketing work may also be evaluated against these following questions and perspectives to determine success.

1. Did the goal sought in this campaign cost less, more or about the same to get the same results as prior campaigns? Did the digital marketer find any new efficiencies or ways to improve on the prior campaign?

2. When the company last tried to reach this audience, how were the metrics measured then as compared to this current campaign? Was this campaign more or less effective than the last time the company sought this audience?

3. If working with new influencers or spokespeople, did the reaction to the influencer reflect well on the brand? Would you use them again?

4. If working with a new digital channel the company has not used before, will more testing be needed before doing a follow-up campaign? How was the ROI compared to previously used channels?

5. If working with a new creative agency or consultant on the content, are there areas of the campaign where success or failure relied on this content quality? Would you use this agency or consultant again?

6. Looking ahead, will there be conditions or approaches in the next six months that would prevent you from continuing this campaign (elections, end of year earnings reports and so on)? Or, is there a natural end to this campaign tactic?

7. Were the results of this campaign timely? Did they bubble up in bursts or was there steady growth in customer engagement or commitment? Did the campaign take too long to pay off revenue-wise?

8. Do the results suggest any pre-work or prep that would need to be done before this type of campaign should be tried again?

9. Is there anything about the campaign's metrics that suggest its outcome is an outlier result, or its success fell under a confluence of events outside the digital marketer's control?

10. Is the technology upon which the campaign was based going to continue to be current or applicable or will the digital marketing team need to upgrade or switch in the time before another campaign?

Industry examples

In this section are some industry examples of digital marketing campaigns and the public reaction to them. From these you can build your own ideas or learn what pitfalls exist as marketers try to capture the public imagination.

Wonder Woman movie[16]

In early June 2017, the movie *Wonder Woman* broke box-office records for a movie by a female director, grossing $220 million USD globally in the first week,[17] and generating 2.19 million tweets.[18]

Hollywood has long watched social media reactions during the first few weekends of a movie; public word-of-mouth and social reaction often serve as an engine of movie success.

To compare to other movies in the 15–21 May timeframe, according to comScore's PreAct service, *Wonder Woman* had started 47,000 new conversations 12 days before release,[19] the action-comedy *Baywatch* spurred 58,000 four days before its release, *Spider-Man: Homecoming* spurred 26,000 new conversations 47 days before its release.

This is an example of both marketing and grassroots success for *Wonder Woman*. The movie's theme of female empowerment, combined with DC comics fan base and a high-profile actress, Gal Gadot, also tweeting information about the movie, united into a tidal wave of support before it opened, and once people started watching the movie, the viral effect snowballed.

However, it was possible for marketers to dig too much into the memes. An Austin movie theatre offered female-only screenings[20] to show support for girl power and groups of women watching the movie together. It ran afoul of local law in doing so and raised the ire of several plaintiffs who sued. At the time of writing, the matter is not settled. Alamo Drafthouse is offering *Wonder Woman* DVDs to the complainants, education for its staff and the use of the situation as a case study for further marketing efforts.

Oreo cookies[21]

Another Twitter campaign that paid off in brand awareness, followers and buzz was the 'you can still dunk in the dark' Oreo tweet during America's Super Bowl 2013.[22] As Super Bowl television slots attract some of the United States' highest viewing audiences, TV ads are enormously expensive, and often the most creative the industry offers, given the high stakes. Traditional and digital marketers begin planning for this American event months in advance and are often working with budgets of millions of dollars.

Oreo's campaign concept was simple: during the Super Bowl, get customers to talk on social media about which part of the sandwich-style cookie they liked best – the filling or the chocolate biscuit. The company had already started a 100-day Twitter programme where the account responded in real time to daily news events.

So, they ran a regular television ad in the first quarter, and they had a 15-person team at the ready to respond to whatever happened online during the Super Bowl. When the lights at the Mercedes-Benz Superdome in New Orleans went out for 34 minutes due to a power outage in the third quarter, Oreo was ready to post a pithy 'Power out? No problem. You can still dunk in the dark' with a picture of a solitary Oreo cookie.

The result? By the next day, that tweet had been retweeted 15,000 times, and Oreo saw a jump from 2,000 Instagram followers to 36,000. The 'cookie or crème' contest had garnered 16,000 pictures submitted by consumers.

Netflix's Stranger Things series and Kellogg's Eggo waffles[23]

Another interesting media integration example for the Super Bowl is Netflix's original programme, *Stranger Things*, which is set in a fictionalised 1980s American town. Kellogg's Eggo waffles had been a consistent product placement in the series, but for season two, the two companies worked together to obtain a one-two punch for consumers. *Stranger Things*' SuperBowl ad began like a 1980s 'Leggo My Eggo' 1980s nostalgia ad for the toaster waffle brand, which was chillingly interrupted by the actual promo for *Stranger Things*. The combo-brand ad got 307,000 tweets during the game and the bantering tweets Eggo prepared for the campaign generated 9,000 retweets and 20,000 likes. As of September 2018, the *Stranger Things*/Eggo ad itself had 17 million views on YouTube.[24]

Natural Environment Research Council's 'Boaty McBoatface'[25]

Popularity and virality can have mixed results. The Natural Environment Research Council (NERC) decided to open the naming of a new ship to the British public in March 2016. This ultra-modern research vessel was being built for £200 million to study ice sheets, ocean currents and marine life in the Antarctic.

The shipbuilding captured the public's imagination – and the British sense of humour.

After former BBC radio presenter James Hand suggested 'Boaty McBoatface' the British public responded in a manner befitting their sense of humour, but not in the way the NERC had intended.[26]

The top five suggestions with votes were:

1. RRS Boaty McBoatface – 124,109
2. RRS Poppy-Mai – 34,371

3.   RRS Henry Worsley – 15,231
4.   RRS It's Bloody Cold Here – 10,679
5.   RRS David Attenborough – 10,284

Ultimately, the ship was named the 'RRS Sir David Attenborough', though one of its remote-operated sub-sea vehicles would be called 'Boaty' in honour of the top vote.[27]

On the one hand, the campaign was an enormous success, with the public clearly engaged, and the submission/voting site overloaded at times. On the other hand, the free-form crowdsourcing of the name and its subsequent popularity meant that NERC really did not have control of its brand. Having an exploratory vehicle carry the popular name, while the boat kept on with the dignified ship-naming tradition (as well as honouring the well-known naturalist Attenborough), was a judicious compromise that saved the day. Still, a savvy digital marketer might have structured the campaign or the naming ritual differently, to spare the government agency grief.

McDonald's – Filet o' Fish sandwiches[28]

Being pitch-perfect around content can make or break success in social media, and in 2017 UK audiences saw a fast food pitch from McDonald's they didn't like. Public reaction to the television commercial was negative and the advertising authority in the UK received 257 complaints about the commercial. Ultimately, McDonald's pulled the ad within four days but not before thousands of people saw a grieving boy, yearning for a connection to his dead father, perking up when eating a Filet o' Fish sandwich upon being told it was his father's favourite.

The strongest action – complaint to the government – arose in tandem with social complaints; the McDonald's ad earned a total of 2,000 social media mentions before it was pulled, with the highest number arising on the day it was pulled. Almost 60 per cent of those mentions were negative.

129

Pepsi ad with Kendall Jenner[29]

Global brand Pepsi made a serious misstep in the spring of 2017 with its ad featuring Kendall Jenner. Celebrities, influencers and regular customers mocked the ad spot, which featured protester Jenner making nice with a riot police officer by handing him a Pepsi and instantly peace broke out. After hearing of the backlash, Pepsi pulled the ad to prevent further brand damage and apologised to the actress for its impact on her career.

The ad, seen as belittling the Black Lives Matter movement, generated 427,000 mentions on Twitter, Facebook and Instagram, a little over half of which were negative. The ad was pulled within three days.

Pepsi's gaffe serves as a reminder that tapping into the zeitgeist and assessing ever-changing public sentiment are both skills and art to the digital marketer. In the United States, increasing social tensions around politics, race, immigration, health care and climate change means that brands must be more careful than usual not to trigger an intense emotional response. What might have been shrugged at, considered funny or appropriate can change swiftly as news breaks. While the ability to capitalise on rapidly emerging memes is an advantage for the digital marketer, the marketer can also find the winds of social perception working against the campaign that seemed so on-point and effective before.

Southern Rail – Eddie the intern

Sometimes, a winning combination (or an affable digital marketing worker) isn't enough. Southern Rail's problems – delayed and cancelled trains, company disputes – were temporarily forgotten as it placed a 15-year-old on work experience at the helm of their Twitter account in July 2017.

His initial, introductory tweet – 'Hi, Eddie here! Here on Work Experience and ready to answer your questions! :)'[30] – at the time of writing, has been shared more than 2,000 times and liked 6,000 times. Eddie went on to answer hypothetical questions about ducks, fajitas and sports – really, anything but the labour disputes and timetable changes Southern Rail was having.[31] Southern Rail saw the fun customers had with the intern and his more light-hearted messages, and instead of clamping down let the relationships build and the positive PR continue.

The problem with the Eddie the intern approach is that eventually Southern Rail's customers turned back to the genuine issues they had with the company, and the real-world problems the railway's delays and cancellations created. Although Eddie was given free rein to engage with customers on many topics during his work experience week, he was not empowered to solve customer service issues or other actions that would benefit the bottom line of the company overall. If the only goal of Southern Rail was brand perception, this approach was a win. If the railway network has a longer-term goal of customer relationships – based on the actual product relationship customers have with Southern Rail – Eddie was only a stopgap measure.

Nivea deodorant – 'White is Purity' campaign[32]

Originally aimed at customers in the Middle East, but visible to 19 million fans on its Facebook page in April 2017, Nivea's 'White is Purity' campaign lasted a few days before the post came down with an apology from Nivea. The company did not respond quickly enough to contain brand damage. By that point, alt-right, and white supremacist groups in the United States had embraced the slogan and urged their followers to buy Nivea products.

In this case, Nivea's marketers showed bad judgment in developing the ad's arguably racist message, but also in not testing the slogan enough to show them what would be a large backlash against the brand. Adoption by hate and bigotry groups is not a broad enough customer base to dominate the company's marketing message, nor is this the brand perception Nivea wants to express.

Like the Pepsi ad, Nivea's marketers also failed to consider how politics and polarisation on the world stage affects public perception of marketing messages. Where Pepsi's marketing team or agency may have felt it was showing a hipster, in-tune-with-now sentiment and missed the mark, here Nivea's marketers arguably showed a degree of white privilege – they failed to think about how people who are not white would react to this marketing message about whiteness. They also failed to take into account how sensitive racial issues have become to people living in a multi-cultural environment, and did not consider both sides of the equation, nor that companies have to firmly come down on the side of equality in their messaging to avoid being perceived as bigoted or discriminatory.

Digital marketers, particularly those intending to reach a global, multi-cultural and multi-ethnic audience, would do well to research and gain an understanding of their audiences' perspective as they evaluate future and past marketing campaigns.

Walkers Crisps – 'Walkers Wave' campaign

If marketing managers give free rein to the online community, there is a strong chance that they will not be happy with the results of the campaign. In May 2017, Walkers Crisps created a campaign for consumers to win tickets for the 'Walkers Wave' UEFA Champions League final football match. Popular ex-footballer, and eater of Walkers Crisps, Gary Lineker, was pictured in online videos on Twitter holding up a card with an image and commenting 'Nice selfie.'[33]

Walkers had asked people to send in selfies using the 'WalkersWave' hashtag which was automatically included in each video. The Match of the Day host appeared in the video holding up a picture of the image in his hands. Unfortunately for Walkers, some people on Twitter responded, not by submitting selfies but by posting images of serial killer Harold Shipman, murderers Fred West and Joseph Fritzel, and disgraced celebrity Jimmy Savile amongst others. Along with legitimate selfies with the hashtag, these images were also displayed on a screen at the football stadium in Cardiff. The videos were removed from the Walkers Crisps Twitter account after a few hours and the company apologised for its activity.

If a digital marketer wants to run a campaign that automatically posts to an online channel, they would do well to ensure that the campaign output is constantly monitored. There will always be those with the intention to disrupt.

SUMMARY

This chapter has walked you through a lengthy array of tools, platforms, techniques and examples of digital marketing campaigns. Now that you see more of the kinds of problems (and solutions!) digital marketers encounter, you will be more readily able to compose your own plans for helping your business to succeed.

Times change, and so will the techniques and technologies you encounter in your daily work. By focusing on the essential components of each approach and marketing framework, insights will remain evergreen even as you update and improve your skills continually. You can learn from examples from the past, but we expect you will find your own playbook and experiments with your campaigns to be just as insightful.

4 NEXT STEPS FOR THE DIGITAL MARKETER

This chapter looks at career progression for the digital marketer. It also suggests how a digital marketer might specialise in one area or another, rather than try to master everything at once; and how to rise to more senior, managerial roles.

DIGITAL MARKETING ROLES

There are many marketing roles and the job titles can seem bewildering to the newcomer. However, there are fundamental functions that these roles perform (these are explored in more detail under their specific role titles in this section) such as content marketing and direct marketing. Let's start with the main roles in digital marketing, before drilling down into differing specialities.

Marketing qualifications

Companies often employ graduates who have taken a marketing related degree. However, there are also other subjects that are very useful to the aspiring marketer:

- Candidates who have taken a course focusing on journalism are considered appropriate for a marketing role, as are graduates of creative design.

- Graduates of media and communications are welcomed in marketing, as are specialists in advertising. If you have taken a business or technology related qualification – or an e-business or e-commerce one – then you will be welcomed into the marketing industry.

- With the rise of big data, data analysts and data scientists are snapped up by companies eager to lead the pack – as are graduates with maths, science and psychology degrees.

Entry-level roles

There are many ways that you can get experience in digital marketing; it does not have to be through formal paths such as degrees or study courses. There are several entry roles you can consider and some are included in this section.

Volunteer social media marketer

An effective way to get a basic understanding of marketing is to volunteer your time at a charity or community organisation. Often, they do not have the skills nor budget to pay for a permanent member of staff. Volunteers will gain valuable practical experience, knowledge about the organisation and learn skills about coordination and social media management.

Digital marketing intern

Some companies offer a paid internship for social media interns or digital marketer graduates who are tempted into the company during the university 'milk rounds' – companies that visit university career fairs each year to showcase job opportunities at the organisation. Often interns have finished their university degree in marketing and want to gain practical experience at a company. They will be given a one or two-year internship, learning about the business and the role of marketing. Once they have completed their time at the company, they can find another role at the company or move to a different organisation.

Digital marketing assistant

Digital marketing assistants will help the marketing manager and team with all marketing activities. They will be expected to submit content for social media campaigns and ensure that any social interactions are responded to in a timely manner.

They will also be expected to write interesting and relevant content for the website and copy for other marketing materials and write marketing communications, uploading them to online social media sites and relevant internet forums.

They will also be responsible for supporting events and exhibitions, booking the venues and coordinating the promotional materials. They will be expected to give support to the rest of the marketing team at promotional events or campaigns.

They will also be responsible for curating and collating material that can be used in promotional literature and managing the marketing department's internal documentation.

Digital marketing coordinator

A typical entry-level role for the digital marketer is usually that of the marketing coordinator or executive. Typically, they are required to work under the direction of someone.

Entry-level digital marketing coordinators or executives are expected to ensure that all enquiries or leads are followed up. They must help to plan marketing communications campaigns, conduct market research and organise promotional marketing events. They must learn how to construct campaigns using the full set of marketing tools available to them. With oversight, they are responsible for writing copy for all marketing resources across the brand including the website, newsletter, blog and physical collateral.

They will be required to work with customers and suppliers, liaising with the brand to make sure every component is progressing well. They should create specifications for customer personas and product specifications. They should also produce competitor analysis reports showing competitor product comparisons and opportunities for own brand promotion.

The online marketing coordinator or executive is focused on maximising marketing opportunities across a variety of channels such as blogs, social media channels and the website. They will ensure that all online content is optimised for search engine marketing and adjusted to fit well across online channels such as Instagram, Facebook or Twitter. The coordinator or executive will handle the social listening campaign, ensuring that any company or brand comments are responded to within the agreed timeframe documented in the media plan. They will engage with customers when proper, keeping an appropriate tone and voice.

They will curate and manage the content calendar, making sure that content is published on a regular basis to ensure brand visibility. They will act as the content ambassador making sure that all content has the appropriate tone of voice for the company.

They will monitor statistics to ensure that all campaigns including pay-per-click (PPC), email marketing and SEO deliver a measurable ROI and use these performance indicators to suggest changes to campaigns.

Roles requiring marketing experience

In this section, you will see an array of roles that assume the applicant already has prior traditional marketing experience, or prior digital experience at minimum.

Digital marketing executive

The digital marketing executive with more experience than an entry level marketer or university graduate, might work more closely with the marketing manager to ensure that the strategy is delivered as per the overall company initiatives. They are required to plan campaigns, manage budgets and agencies, and handle other management aspects of the strategy. They should monitor campaign spend so discrepancies and variances against the budget can be highlighted. (In the United States, this job might be called marketing *coordinator.*)

A more experienced digital marketing executive who has already carried out a range of marketing activities must deliver the company marketing strategy for a product or brand, making sure that other teams within the company are aware of marketing efforts. They are still a doer but are trusted with more autonomy.

They should prepare a wide range of marketing materials including online materials and physical collateral. However, as they are not entry level, they may be able to delegate this work to a more junior digital marketing executive or coordinator.

They must create strategies to drive traffic to the website and plan and manage digital marketing campaigns using paid search, PPC and SEO. They must coordinate any marketing activity with sales initiatives and maintain a content calendar and publishing timeline. They must improve lead generation and measure, monitor and report on the results of campaigns.

They should also be able to accurately report on total spend per campaign, providing analysis and reports to make sure that campaigns operate successfully. They might also be asked to research new opportunities for the brand and analyse campaigns for failures and successes.

They will be required to carry out research of both market activity and competitors to ensure that the company can uncover opportunities for the brand.

They must help to manage the brand and product campaigns and improve the design and content of the website. Experienced digital marketing executives know to keep ahead of technology developments and, if working with an agency, manage the client relationship to ensure that campaigns meet expectations.

They may also be required to investigate partner relationships for partner marketing campaigns.

Digital marketing manager

Digital marketing managers have a variety of roles according to the type of company they work for. They are responsible for managing the marketing for the company, and for ensuring that the marketing strategy and online campaigns are delivered in line with the company vision, on budget and on time. They are responsible for the management and identity of the brand or company.

They handle planning and managing digital marketing campaigns and make sure that their company remains at the forefront of digital marketing technologies. They will also keep an eye on the current market conditions including information on competitor activities and carry out regular customer research surveys to ensure that satisfaction and perception about the brand continues to be positive.

If their role includes looking after the company website, then the marketing manager will be responsible for driving traffic to it. They will manage any redesign of the website, ensuring that conversion rates improve because of the improvements made. They will also manage the content of the site, looking at usability and design. If the company does not employ an SEO specialist, then the marketing manager will use paid search, PPC and SEO techniques to improve site visibility on search engines.

Digital marketing managers may serve as managers to the digital marketing executives and guide the strategic decisions that their direct reports implement. Generally, they work within the marketing department or in a subsection of the marketing department.

But what if you want to go even further in your career – up the ladder to where you are leading large teams or even managing leaders of those teams? If cross-company impact is on your radar, read the next section.

Senior marketing roles

Companies can structure digital marketing organisations as a separate unit or combine them with other marketing teams under one leadership team or executive. In this section we include several of the roles for the highest levels of digital marketing.

Obviously, if applying for one of these jobs, pay special attention to how the reporting structures are described, and what teams the role is responsible for leading, as titles can vary from company to company.

Head of marketing

The head of marketing will have multiple disciplines to manage as well as the task of creating the vision for the rest of the marketing team. They must consider all parts of management across the marketing organisation. They will lead their team of digital marketers to implement their strategy through paid media and earned media such as blogs, forums and other social media which they use to create opportunities for the company.

They work closely with the marketing director, to make sure that the company has an effective marketing strategy, and will regularly report on all activities to them. The head of marketing will also work closely with other departmental leads on corporate initiatives and marketing projects, making sure that all campaigns and projects represent brand guidelines and adhere to the overall marketing strategy.

The head of marketing will represent the company at industry events and watch trends to make sure the company is at the forefront of digital marketing in their field.

They will recruit members of the marketing team and make sure that the team is resourced properly to carry out the company strategy. They will also have a compete strategy to make sure that the company is performing well in the market.

At a company where traditional marketing is separate from the digital arm, the head of marketing reports on all activities to the director of digital marketing and works closely with other parts of the organisation to make sure that the marketing and communications strategies are continually developed and delivered when required.

Director of digital marketing

The director of digital marketing works closely with the head of marketing to make sure that an effective marketing strategy has been developed and is in place across the organisation. The director has overall responsibility for the organisation's marketing activities and ensures that the development and delivery of the marketing strategy is integrated across the whole business, whilst making sure that day-to-day activities across the organisation are carried out in accordance with the integrated marketing strategy.

The director oversees all marketing activities to ensure that the team fulfils the company marketing strategy and considers new and emerging products to include in the marketing mix. They work with the sales team to ensure that commercial objectives are met by the activities of the marketing team. They also look at the competitive landscape to analyse it and consumer buying trends.

The director of digital marketing will oversee the implementation of the all-up marketing strategy, all the campaigns, events and PR outreach strategies, ensuring that materials, presentations and literature are provided to the sales teams and other departments.

The director of digital marketing is responsible for the brand and how well it performs commercially. They are also responsible for the brand's customers, strategy and objectives. Cross-team collaboration across the organisation is a business imperative for the director as is building the brand and being an ambassador for the brand internally, and externally. They work with the product teams to define marketing materials and sales programmes and direct the social media marketing team to create programmes to improve customer satisfaction and perception about the brand.

Director of digital

The digital marketing director handles the all-up online marketing strategy and brand awareness. They create the company plan in line with its overall mission and vision, and create the marketing plan. They will ensure that the marketing budget is distributed across all online campaigns and that the strategy is carried out in accordance with product development and release dates. They will ensure that the marketing team performs to stated KPIs and will use analytics tools and dashboards to ensure that the company has a measurable ROI.

The director's team will use social media, outbound campaigns such as PPC and email campaigns to drive traffic to the website and increase its visibility in search results. They will also be responsible for team outcomes, ecommerce and generating online leads for the sales team to action.

Should the digital function be scattered across the marketing organisation or company divisions, a director of digital would also be responsible for leading the entire digital marketing team across the business.

CAREER PROGRESSION

There are several ways that you can get onto the first step of the marketing ladder. There are also many ways of advancing your digital marketing career.

Digital marketers need to embody a 'growth mindset' – that is, seeking continuously to learn, even through failures, and relishing the challenge of mastering a new skill. This concept, taken from a book called *Mindset* by Carol Dweck,[1] is especially crucial for a digital marketer because the digital marketing landscape is continually changing.

Each new campaign is an experiment, pushing the boundaries of what is possible for the company the digital marketer works for. Every new opportunity demands that the digital marketer uses their skills to the best of their ability, even as those skills expand.

It is important to remember that organisations can vary in their structure for accommodating digital marketing activities, and where some of the different marketing roles might sit. For example, some organisations might sit social media in the PR team and keep the broadcast marketing channels separate from online marketing. This can be further complicated when organisations have in-house marketing teams rather than use agencies, and those companies that combine the two. Marketing skillsets may be similar but the roles themselves can vary dramatically.

Some digital marketing roles may not even reference the term 'digital marketing' itself. For example, a corporate communications coordinator job title could incorporate a role focused on website, internal communications, social media, email and content marketing.

Do you want to work for a company or an agency?

Who will you serve as a digital marketer? Do you favour going in deep, to one company or one product, with an identity bound up in that brand? Or do you fancy yourself a digital creative and nomad, working on new challenges for new companies on a continuous basis? This next section explores working for a company vs. working for an agency.

Company

If you like the challenge of working to develop a brand or suite of brands, then consider becoming an in-house digital marketer. Here you will be able to develop a thorough knowledge of the brand, product or service. You will develop a relationship with the product team as they work to finalise the product for your team to market. Your campaign will need to be pitched across

143

the business to ensure that it satisfies the company 'voice' and will enhance sales of the product without compromising sales of another product at the company.

Your challenge will be to secure budget for your campaign. Often budgets are allocated annually and divided quarterly. You will need to work with the product teams to ensure that your remaining budget matches the product release schedule for the financial year. You will be asked to prove that your campaign delivers a strong marketing ROI and convince stakeholders at different levels of the organisation that your marketing budget for the campaign will be well spent, and company objectives satisfied.

See Figure 4.1 for common brand roles within a company.

Figure 4.1 Brand roles within a company

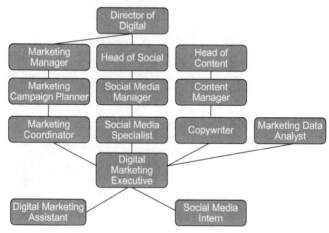

Agency

Agencies work in fast moving, dynamic environments with a variety of clients and a plethora of products. No two days are the same and the job certainly isn't boring. Both creative and data roles feature significantly in digital marketing activities. You will be responsible for developing and pitching ideas to the client and driving them towards a decision. You will need to be skilled at negotiating costs, timelines, deadlines and teams needed for the job. Then, as the project takes shape, you will be responsible for managing the project – and the people on the client side. You will need to be able to resolve issues quickly and move the project forward to a successful end.

You will develop a close relationship with your client, but bear in mind that sometimes agency clients or directors demand a viral campaign without truly understanding what that is and how it comes about. Diplomacy and tact are key.

You will also need to make sure that you are up to speed with all the latest technologies and innovations, marketing trends and emerging media. You will be the expert for the duration of the project or projects, so you need to make sure that you can deliver.

See Figure 4.2 for common roles within an agency.

Figure 4.2 Agency roles

Gaining on-the-job knowledge and experience

You need to understand the marketing industry. You might know your own role, and the roles on your team or department, but how does this function fit in with other roles in similar industries?

Network with other marketing professionals like yourself. Ask them questions about their roles and the sort of campaigns they run. Look at online discussion groups such as the Marketing, Sales, Social Media, and PR Innovators network[2] or the Social Media Marketing Group[3] on LinkedIn – viewable to logged on LinkedIn users. You can learn from following companies such as the American Marketing Association[4] or groups like the Chartered Institute of Marketing or the UK Marketing Network.[5] Following discussions on LinkedIn and other such professional channels will help you to learn the fundamentals of your role and will also give you tips and advice on how to move forward.

You may be required to manage staff as you progress through your career. If you have never managed a team before it is a good idea to brush up on the skills you might need to become a manager. You will need to work on your style of management, your leadership skills and how you interact with people and other teams in the company. You will also need to be resilient and assertive and have the right personality to become a manager.

If you manage multi-channel campaigns already, you are well on the way to taking the next step in your career. You do, however, need to understand how your marketing role fits in with the wider organisation or business. You also need to be able to define the overall business objective of your role to senior managers. Have you measured a variety of online metrics and presented them to a board member or senior manager with confidence? Have you defined any criteria to help you understand whether you have achieved any of your campaign objectives? If you can ensure that you can deliver these with confidence, then you are ready to move onto the next step of your career.

CHOOSING YOUR PATH

There are many different paths that you may choose to take as a digital marketer and, once working in a marketing role, you can often change focus and move to a different type of specialism. Generally, marketers start their career at a junior level, and as they gain expertise decide to follow one specific marketing discipline.

Affiliate marketing roles

Affiliate marketers develop affiliate marketing programmes and provide analytics and reports about online sales. Affiliate marketing rewards its affiliates for driving customers to the website to purchase. It relies on people promoting links to the website on their own websites or social media platforms. Affiliate marketers need to stay up to date on software and trends and make sure that their website appeals to customers. Affiliate marketers work closely with SEO, PPC, SEM, social media marketers and direct marketers.

See Figure 4.3 for common affiliate marketing roles within a company.

Figure 4.3 Affiliate marketing roles

Content roles

In digital marketing, content is king, so content roles are key to delivering a successful strategy. Writing good copy is key for the web. Creating engaging video and other media will ensure that all website content is effective and brings customers to the site. Content must be optimised for SEO using keywords and produced for different social channels using the corporate tone and voice. It is usual for content to be delivered in line with a content calendar that aligns with the marketing initiatives and overall company vision. Content must also be optimised for engaging and entertaining direct marketing campaigns.

See Figure 4.4 for common content roles within a company.

Figure 4.4 Content roles

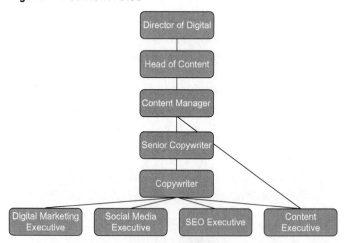

Communications roles

The communications team is responsible for developing the integrated strategy and overall communications ('comms') budget for the company. It is tasked with increasing brand awareness, reputation and satisfaction. It must develop relationships with media outlets, write press releases and try to generate positive coverage in online and offline channels. Digital marketers specialising in communications also need to monitor news about the company and analyse sentiment in case a crisis management plan needs to be actioned.

The team will have to communicate brand values to internal stakeholders across the business and lead the communications strategy for the company.

See Figure 4.5 for common communication roles within a company.

Figure 4.5 Comms roles

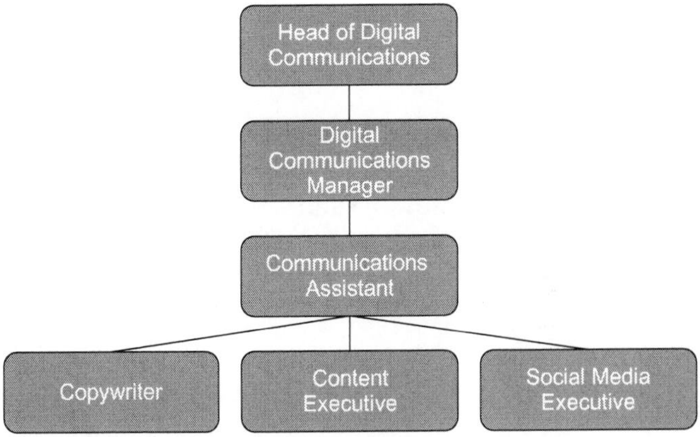

Customer relationship management roles

The CRM team must ensure that CRM provides an effective sales funnel and an efficient sales mechanism. The CRM system must be customer focused, correctly segmented and deliver relevant marketing messages to the customers to ensure a positive ROI. The team must work with agencies, partners, suppliers and across the whole business to make sure that the strategy and plan are delivered appropriately.

See Figure 4.6 for common CRM roles within a company.

Figure 4.6 CRM roles

Direct or email marketing roles

Direct or email marketers are responsible for managing all the outbound marketing campaigns using direct email marketing. They will be responsible for the content of all emails sent to customers either on a regular basis or triggered by a customer action such as a renewal or sale. They will make continual improvement to their marketing campaigns based on the analysis of their reports. They will carry out A/B testing to ensure that the most effective campaign goes to the right section of their audience. They will segment their audience to ensure that the correct content goes to the correct customer or potential customer.

They will track the success of open rates and bounce rates to ensure that links are valid, and are clicked, and that content is compelling enough for the customer to signal intent to buy.

They will create reports on campaign success in terms of sales, and make sure that all email campaigns are operated legally and in compliance with the Advertising Standards Authority code of practice.

They will work with the CRM team to ensure that there is a strategy and process in place to manage new and returning customers to ensure the highest levels of customer satisfaction, recommending improvements where necessary.

See Figure 4.7 for common direct or email marketing roles within a company.

Figure 4.7 Direct marketing roles

Display advertising roles

Display advertisers focus on delivering adverts to the customer across a variety of digital channels such as those mentioned in the previous chapter.

See Figure 4.8 for common display advertising roles within a company.

Pay-per-click roles

PPC roles drive clicks and calls to action (CTAs) to the website and media campaigns. Search engine marketers and website

Figure 4.8 Display advertising roles

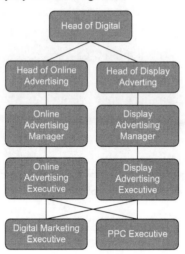

optimisers pay search engines to promote their websites by making sure they have good visibility in search engine results. They ensure that their sites have an appropriate number of keywords and links for search engine bots to index. These keywords might include title tags, heading tags, meta tags and image Alt. tags. They will also have knowledge in back-end analytics tools to show the measurement of success of the website and paid ad.

> Web analytics and validation tools are valuable in showing how each page on a website is performing and whether there are any problems that need to be addressed.

See Figure 4.9 for common PPC roles within a company.

Figure 4.9 PPC roles

SEO and SEM roles

SEO and SEM roles tend to concentrate on elevating the company or its campaign materials in search engine results. For example, the company's website, the landing page for a new product, a key marketing video – all of these may benefit from SEO techniques. Likewise, strategically placed search ad buys on related topics – where users will be of the mind to click on the company's product or service – are a foundational tool for enhancing awareness.

See Figure 4.10 for common SEO and SEM roles within a company.

Social media roles

Social media digital marketing roles manage customer engagement, perception and company reputation through the successful use of earned media.

See Figure 4.11 for common social media roles within a company.

Figure 4.10 SEO roles

Figure 4.11 Social media roles

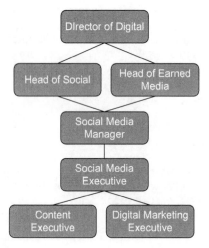

Entrepreneurial roles

Entrepreneurial marketers may decide to go it alone and work for themselves. They are then responsible for the whole business. They need to understand day-to-day operations as well as the legal, tax and financial processes needed to run their own business. They also need to market themselves effectively to secure work as well as deliver what the client wants them to do. Some marketers run digital agencies, some are consultants working for a variety of customers and some are trainers, delivering workshops on behalf of a brand.

Social media consultant

The social media consultant must always look to the next opportunity, whilst demonstrating their excellence at their current assignment and keeping their business – and associates if they have them – busy with work.

Digital agency manager

Agency managers should be able to provide their clients with insights about their products and produce optimised promotions and plans for the client. They must develop strong relationships with the marketing team at the client, as well as the merchandising team. They will need to be able to work alongside the client account team to create strategies and optimise campaigns to improve brand performance. They will be required to work with customers, and suppliers, liaising with the brand to make sure every component of a campaign is progressing well.

They might also need to manage analysts and marketing support teams to deliver campaigns across a range of related merchandising.

Digital agency director

Digital agency directors make sure that the company services including PPC, social media marketing, reputation monitoring, digital crisis management and programmatic media campaigns are carried out for customers. They manage a team of creative, energised and lively staff who often work long hours.

They will oversee all clients and campaigns, ensuring their team of agency managers deliver the collective vision for the agency. They will make sure all the stakeholders at the agency are fully briefed on the direction that the agency is to take.

CONTINUOUS PROFESSIONAL DEVELOPMENT

One of the most talked about subjects in professional circles is the digital skills gap. Digital marketing is one of the key areas where there is a real risk of that gap growing. More and more channels, such as IoT, open opportunities before some digital marketers have even got a good grasp on how to market across existing channels. This digital skills gap can be addressed with continuous professional development (CPD).

Companies sometimes want their candidates to be qualified to a professional level. The Chartered Institute of Marketing[6] offers several levels of qualifications. These qualifications vary from a foundation certificate in marketing to a marketing leadership programme, equivalent to a master's degree.

Taking CPD courses adds credits to your formal qualifications and ensures that all your courses, training and private studies are documented.

In addition to professional qualifications and training courses, there are other ways for digital marketers to continuously develop – attending industry events, volunteering to mentor a less experienced marketer and sharing experience through blogging or on digital marketing forums are just a few examples.

The CPD certification service[7] ensures that learning is 'conscious and proactive' instead of 'passive and reactive'. It means that marketers can keep their practical qualifications and are continually updated their skills and remaining relevant.

SUMMARY

Now that you have seen the various specialisations and seniority levels open to you as a digital marketer, we hope that you will better be able to plan for a long and happy career in the field. Continued learning and education opportunities, professional associations and conferences, and ongoing research will help you rise through the ranks.

5 A DAY IN THE LIFE OF A DIGITAL MARKETER

What will it really be like you ask? This chapter explores those questions by following the fictitious business intern Carl, as he tries to execute his duties and learn more about digital marketing.

This case study is based on the real-life business experiences of the two authors, carefully woven together to create the most insightful narrative. As you might expect, many companies will have only some of these roles, depending on need, but we wanted a narrative where Carl could encounter the most examples.

You can see from this example that Carl is only given one piece of the digital marketing puzzle at his company, and other co-workers and mentors see the problem from different angles. Not all businesses are the size of this 'company X' and not all business will need multiple digital marketing channels. Still, this 'day in the life' scenario should help a nascent digital marketer to get a sense of the day-to-day activities of the profession.

Because digital marketers can be found at all levels of a company, and each has their role to play, this composite case study will look at how different digital marketers interact with each other inside company X, which makes three separate lines of household goods. We will focus on and follow the day of a digital marketing intern, Carl, who will be returning to university studies in the autumn but who has a boss who is determined that he should see what the job is really like.

CASE STUDY: CARL AT 'COMPANY X'

Carl, the entry level social media intern for his digital marketing team, starts the workday by checking dashboards and alert emails from the company's three Twitter accounts – customer support, the main company brand handle and the third one from the company CEO. Satisfied that no PR crises erupted during his off-hours, he sends an email to his boss, Abby, who is his mentor for the summer, and responsible for seeing that he experiences many sides of the business.

'So far, last night's announcement for a sale on bed sheets today has had 100 retweets from our diehard influencers, with an impact of 550,000 impressions total', his email reads. 'The customer support Twitter handle only dealt with two complaints about running out of the black lampshades. I think we have weathered that storm.'

'Good,' Abby replies. 'Today I am expecting you to prepare the scheduled tweets for the rest of the sale week on linens, ending Friday. Run them by me when you are done.'

Carl sets to work. By noon, he has nine proposed tweets – three for each of the remaining three days of the week – and Abby has pointed out places to change wording for brand messaging and brevity. He sets up the nine scheduled tweets ready to go in his social media management tool, so they automatically remind followers in the morning, noon when they may take a lunch break to go shopping, and right before the close of the business day when they may be thinking about shopping after work.

Abby has arranged for the two of them to have lunch with another digital marketer in the company, Francesca, a director who works with video agencies and other multimedia vendors. Francesca came to digital marketing after stints in filmmaking and agency creative work – she has enjoyed working with company X because her acumen and shrewd eye for costs can help to make a campaign successful at a lower budget.

Over salad and sandwiches, Francesca questions Carl about his university studies, and then asks him about his experiences.

'I did a podcast with a friend briefly in my second year of university,' he admits, 'it was about science fiction movies and anime. We got 30,000 downloads a month before we got too busy to keep it up. It was fun, but a lot of work!'

Francesca nods. 'Those are good numbers for something you do in your spare time,' she said. 'One of our competitors has about 200,000 total views for their video on how to fold neat corners when making a bed – we need to get our how-to videos to at least that number to get our sheets in front of as many people.'

Carl jots down something in his notebook, a prompt to think about video later. 'Perhaps I can come up with some ideas,' he said. 'But I'm curious – what else do you do besides analyse other company's videos?'

Francesca chews a bite of sandwich as she thinks, then answers, 'As director I lead a team that has to handle all the incoming requests for multimedia marketing collateral. This means all my people must be involved or at least aware of our company's branding strategies, design guidelines and what the latest channels and campaigns will be. I might have one person working on a digital ad to be shown on Facebook, and another person taking an even shorter version of that ad to be woven in to videos on YouTube.'

'I have a set budget and video is expensive to produce – possibly in the millions if you have a celebrity, expensive location and multiple setting or language variations on the video that has to go out. So, my job is also to figure out where best to put that money. Just like you do for Abby, I have one person just focused on getting out the metrics reports, daily and weekly, so that our team can decide whether to pull a video down or not.'

'So, you are not sitting on film sets yelling "Cut!" all day long?' Carl grins.

Francesca laughs. 'No, but I am always trying to figure out ways we can do it a bit cheaper or get more out of what we have. You can shoot video with an iPhone now, so how-to videos don't have to be of the highest production quality.'

After lunch, Abby takes Carl to see the head of email marketing at the company, a marketing manager named Stu. Stu has been working as a digital marketer for five years since he graduated, starting as someone writing email marketing copy and then working his way up to leading the company-wide efforts.

'The company's newsletter email list is a very important responsibility,' Stu tells Carl. 'For one thing, depending on the laws where the email is sent, if we do not properly let people opt in or out of the mailings, we will have lawyers chasing us in a heartbeat. But the other thing is to watch the open, click-through and conversion rates carefully for each campaign; have a control mechanism in place; and a treatment or experiment happening so that the marketing can improve based on the results of the campaign compared to the controlled experiment. For example, our customers respond better to "Egyptian cotton" mentions in the advertising copy more than the thread count, which was surprising. I think maybe it's because they know we will have a high thread count already, so it is the softness and quality of the fibre that draws them in.'

'The other thing we test is calls to action in the subject lines,' Stu says. 'See here – these are the ones that get the money word like "free" or "discount" in the first part of the subject line. These are the ones that will get the markdown item – king-sized and double sheet sets – as the first part of the subject line. Each time we update our customers, we are testing to figure out what they want to hear from us and the way they want to hear it.'

Carl peers at Stu's large monitor screen. 'Looks complicated,' he says.

'Not really,' Stu says. 'It's just unfamiliar to you, and each email vendor will be different. But they all will have to provide editing tools and they all should provide metrics reporting so you can see whether your messaging broke through.'

Carl scratches his head and thinks about his college friends. 'I thought people were moving away from email,' he says. 'Isn't everyone on chat software by now?'

Abby breaks in, 'Sure, and we can market to those chat platforms as well. But email marketing continues to be a strong mechanism for creating a relationship with a customer, and it does not depend on them being online at the time the message was sent. Also, Stu here can fine-tune his email messaging to only certain kinds of newsletter subscribers or purchasers. It really depends on what works best for each company and, in our case, our high-end buyers really want to hear about sheet sales via email newsletters that make them feel catered to.'

'If we wanted to hit a demographic – like millennials or generation Z – we would consider what social platforms they are using this year and target to those,' Stu says. 'I think Abby has you working on Twitter now because you can see really rapidly and in real time what the effects of the company's messages are, but later in the summer we can have you work on broadening the company's base to those newer audiences and channels.'

Carl looks excited. 'I've got at least three places online that my friends are on, but our company is not,' he grins.

Abby and Stu exchange looks. 'Just remember, the channels you open for the company must be sustainable,' Abby reminds Carl. 'You get to go back to university in two months, but we need to make sure there is a staff member here able to handle the channels, or we could annoy our potential customers by neglecting them when they contact us. We don't want to be caught two steps behind everyone else, but we have to ensure the contact is quality, or we shouldn't do it.'

'Don't worry,' Carl promises. 'Not only will I do an audience monitoring check like you showed me last week, I can figure out ways to automate it so that the messages from Facebook or Twitter get propagated across the new platforms automatically.'

'Well, I think you've seen enough of the email marketing side of the house for today,' Stu says, 'and I need to get back to my team. But could you take Carl to see Margaret, to give him an even broader view of the digital marketing role?'

Abby checks her phone. 'I think we can nab her, she usually gets a coffee after the Leadership meeting.' She takes Carl to the vice president of PR and marketing's office where Margaret is, as predicted, sipping a coffee and looking over reports.

'Hi Margaret,' Abby says. 'We only want to grab five minutes of your time – this is Carl, the new intern in digital marketing.'

Carl shakes her hand, and Margaret smiles at his earnest expression. 'So, what would you like to know, in this five-minute coffee break?'

Carl blurts out, 'How do I become a VP like you?!'

Abby smiles at that, as the three of them sit down at the small conference table in Margaret's office. 'I'd like to know that too.'

'Well,' Margaret says. 'My path was a little different, because they didn't have digital marketing when I was an intern like you. I worked in a marketing firm, switched to PR for a couple of years, and then came back to a marketing agency where I could handle both PR and marketing for clients. Eventually, I worked my way up to director of marketing at a different company, and then transferred to company X. By this time, digital had already become important; I had created such strong teams under me, my people were explaining to me how we needed to approach the next big wave of social media advertising and marketing.'

'So, you didn't need to understand digital marketing to become vice president?' Carl asks.

Margaret makes a face. 'I don't think that is true anymore,' she says. 'It is too easy for a company to make mistakes or lose sales to their competitor on digital platforms. Even if your specialty in marketing is not digital, you still have to understand how it works.'

She looks out the window, remembering. 'I went to conferences, took classes, and read research reports,' Margaret said. 'Even though my team said not to worry, that they would handle everything – I wanted to be on top of this new exciting way to reach customers. I didn't want to be the figurehead at the top, I wanted to be helping them with strategies that made sense in the new digital age.'

She turns to Abby. 'If you can go deep in digital, or any other area, while still managing to keep the broader perspective – that's how executives are made in this business.'

Abby nods. She is aware that the execs at company X often burn the midnight oil, reading over reports from their people as well as discussing new strategies to keep the business expanding. And her digital team can work all hours too, though she tries to ensure they flex their time enough not to burn out. Tired brains can be quicker to anger, and a cool head is what one needs in online communications. Particularly in a crisis.

Carl meanwhile is excited. 'I'll be taking a digital communications class during the autumn term,' he says. 'It's part project, part exam-based.'

Margaret smiles. 'Keep learning Carl, and you will never lose the spark for this business,' she says. Turning to Abby she says, 'I need to get a presentation ready for the board, so unfortunately this is all the time I have for you. But feel free to have Carl email me at the end of the internship – I want to find out what he's discovered while here.'

As they walk out, Abby whispers, 'Stu and I spent days creating one slide for that report she is presenting. Marketers across the company delivered their reports for the last quarter, and Stu had to corral all of it into a format that Margaret could start working with.'

'Sounds like communication inside the company can take as much time and effort as the stuff we do outside the company.'

'Yes, if you do it right.'

Carl almost bumps into a tall, skinny man in the hallway with square spectacles. 'Oh Carl, this is Louis, who heads up our search engine marketing team,' Abby says. 'Louis, this is Carl our intern – do you have five minutes to chat with him about what you do?'

Louis is carrying a slim folder in his hand. 'If you buy me coffee anything is possible,' he says. 'I do have 20 minutes to spare – let us head for the cafeteria and I can show Carl the latest printouts from our campaigns.'

Louis spreads out his papers in front of Carl.

'I'm not sure I get it,' Carl looks up at him, puzzled. 'It seems like you are guessing how much money and how long your campaigns will be. The other folks seemed to know what deadlines they had and what it costs exactly, say, to make a video.'

Louis laughs. 'I do explain these are projections, but search engine marketing does have caps so that you don't go over budget. But the ad campaigns are really bidding on an auction – and the best price for a keyword on say Google or Bing is the price that gets locked down and paid. So, I don't know for sure I can get all the search terms I want – that's why that sheet over there has the list of all the possible variations we can try if we don't get the terms we want.'

'Search ads are pretty boring,' Carl says. 'They are mostly text links, right? And people are really looking for the search results, not your ad.'

'All this is true, though the search engines are always improving the kinds of ads you can place,' Louis says. 'But search ads, even during the most recent recession, were some of the best performing advertisements around. Can you tell me why that might be?'

Carl frowns. 'They were smaller and cheaper?'

'That may be true, but that's not it,' Louis replies. 'Think about what happens when someone is searching for something. They type words into a search box or may say something to a digital assistant who understands speech. They are on the hunt for something that they want. They are active. And they've given the search engine clues about what it is they want.'

'But places like Facebook can give you demographics, target you based on your likes,' Carl says. 'What's so great about being in the middle of someone's search?'

'If they are trying to buy a good or a service, they are active and ready for you to hand them the answer,' Louis says. 'Your search ad might be more on point in answering what they want than the organic results. And they are, metaphorically speaking, sitting there searching with money in their hands, hoping to find a place to spend it.'

'The other aspect of search engine marketing is making sure our company shows up properly in search results,' Abby says. 'And social media helps this – every time someone tweets the link to our company site, we get the benefit of that traffic and that link in search engine relevance calculations. It's not one-to-one upvoting of course, and there are thousands of signals that search engines use – but keeping our digital content precise and helpful makes it more likely to be shown as a relevant result to someone who doesn't even know our products.'

Carl studies the printouts in front of him. 'It looks like we do analytics for search ads that lead people onto our website,' he says.

'Yes, that is another part of the puzzle: what happens to people once your advertising gets them to your landing page,' Louis smiles. 'I probably have to get these gathered up and get going but stop by my office Friday and you can see the report I created for our executive review. If you like content marketing, there is an emerging role in the industry sometimes called a digital knowledge manager.'

'I don't think I've even heard of this one,' Abby says.

Louis stacks his papers. 'Think of it as having one person or leader act as content coordinator for the whole company; you can ensure your digital data is routed to the right opportunity.'

'For example, what if Carl here does a fun profile of an employee in the internal company newsletter, with photos and text in a digital file. The digital knowledge manager might say, why not re-use that for the company blog, or excerpt from it when the employee speaks at a conference? As more company assets become digital, it opens opportunities that the company will not want to waste. Having a digital knowledge manager – or whatever the title – can be quite useful for larger corporations growing their digital strategy.'

'Wow, that sounds really cool,' Carl says. 'Maybe I should try to work towards that after I graduate.'

'Well, keep your eyes peeled for how the job listings use titles and see what you find,' Louis says. 'Names may change, but the work always needs to get done. I will see you tomorrow!'

Carl and Abby wave goodbye and then walk back to Abby's office. Carl's head is spinning, thinking of all the exciting digital marketing career possibilities.

GLOSSARY

360-degree videos (ads)   These are immersive or spherical video ads that allow the user to pan about the ad experience as in a panorama. Real estate listings and hotel rooms are common uses for this kind of video ad.

A/B testing   Compares two variable audience response options against one marketing campaign. It can determine which variant is the most successful in a campaign based on the response from each audience.

Acquisition cost   This is when customers buy the good or service and officially join the company's customer community. This will vary by mechanism and the demographics of the customer sought after by each business. So, for example, it may be the cost of the advertising campaign divided by the number of successful customers acquired. Or, there may be a digital mechanism built in that automatically tracks and assesses the cost per acquisition. See **Retention metrics**.

Active users   Those who come to a company's site, app or social media outlet and interact in the desired way at least once. Digital marketers, particularly when using games as part of the marketing campaign, often use the acronyms DAU (Daily Active Users) and MAU (Monthly Active Users) to represent these users. A sign of engagement health is that the number of such users increases. See **Engagement metrics**.

Ad serving   Technology that places advertisements on web pages, inside email newsletters, and inside mobile phone texts or apps. Ad serving platforms must be fast, precise and able to adapt to different devices or form factors in serving the proper ads.

Affiliate marketing When a company, blogger or consultancy is paid for referring customers to another business as an affiliate of that business. The business will set reward or incentive levels for its affiliates for giving these referrals or leads (often marked by special online links that measure the pass-through and allow the results to be tracked). A famous early example of this is Amazon's affiliate programme, which gave credit as bloggers and others linked through to product pages on the internet retailer's site.

Agencies Fast moving, dynamic workplaces with a variety of clients and products.

Alt. tag HMTL code to annotate and tag images and video files so that search engines can understand multimedia on web pages. Multimedia captions and descriptive text indicate what the component is.

Analytics platforms These aggregate campaign findings in an easy-to-read format, offering visualisations and summaries or an opportunity to dig deeper into the data.

Approval This term is used to cover various social media mechanisms where the user can indicate an emotion around the digital content being shared by another, or about their own content. Facebook 'likes', for example, are tallied for the visitor when they go to a Facebook page and Facebook can display which of the customer's friend circle also liked the page or product. Facebook has broadened its likes to include angry, sad and other emotions as well as just the classic thumbs up symbol, because the marketing signal here is important to understand. People can share things that outrage them, that they do not support, as well as items they like, and it is not a good idea to confuse the two. Social platforms usually only verify numbers of their own users who like, share or perform another action on a content item or product on their platform, so what the platform offers and what it tracks varies. See **Engagement metrics**.

Attribution modelling A specific touchpoint across the sales process that attributes all, or part, of the credit for the sale to that action.

Audience targeting and segmentation Specific demographics and psychographics to be selected for ad campaigns.

BCS, The Chartered Institute for IT A UK-based organisation founded in 1957 that promotes wider social and economic progress through the advancement of information technology.

Bounce rate The rate at which visitors view a website's home page or a specific page and then leave without exploring the rest of the website. Generally, this is calculated by looking at visitors who saw the page and then took an action to leave: they hit the back button on the web browser or typed in another web address and left, or left the browser window open and never came back to the page (resulting in the user session timing out).

Bounce rate can also be used for landing pages tied to online advertising, blogs, end of trial software offers or other digital presentations of a marketing message or offer. The 'bounce' is the user's choice to leave what has been offered to them throughout the customer journey to conversion. This could be the departure from a web page after a defined time, the departure from the site to make payment, the decision not to open a marketing email addressed to them or a link within that email. Sometimes, an email address is invalid and 'bounces' back to the sender; this is also called a 'bounce rate'. See **Retention metrics**.

Breadth reach The extent to which a piece of marketing content has travelled across different audiences.

Chatbot An app, piece of software or computer program that simulates conversation with a user. This can be rudimentary, matching keywords to canned responses, or in-depth use of artificial intelligence, natural language algorithms and machine learning to allow greater command of syntax and meaning.

Churn The number of customers that leave a site for assorted reasons compared to the number of customers who continue to use the site over the same amount of time.

Click-through rate A comparison made between the number of content items seen (web page impressions, banner ad impressions and so on) and the users' rate of clicking on the link(s) provided by the content to get to the marketing destination.

It is the measure of whether your marketing call to action worked on the intended customer. For online advertising, often click-through rate is represented as 'CTR' and expressed as a percentage. However, in the social media world, there may be other proper responses of engagement. For example, if the digital marketer is offering a discount code which is good for as many people as it is shared with, there is social capital to be had by sharing the discount, and it encourages that sharing. The discount code in this example must be entered at the company's site when buying, and is not a link but is a key part of the call to action. The number of orders using the discount code would show the digital marketer how effective the social media campaign was. If the marketer can understand why visitors click on ads, then they can repeat the success. See **Engagement metrics**.

Content delivery networks (CDNs) A distributed network of servers that have content syndicated to them to ensure delivery of user content from a server closest to them. CDNs reduce page load time and improve the quality of media delivery – especially live-streaming media.

Content management system (CMS) Used to publish content, schedule it and organise it for the viewer.

Content marketing Content marketing is the production of content interesting to your brand's customers.

Contextual targeting Online ads which are displayed in different formats according to the type of device or browser accessing the ad. Used to ensure the reader has the best ad experience across devices and platforms.

Conversion The act of turning a potential customer into an actual customer. Getting users to convert is the true value of a website. Measurement of conversion depends on the desired outcome of the marketing campaign and the level of commitment needed to obtain it (a purchase of a good or service, giving up an email address to subscribe to a newsletter, watching an online seminar trial pitch and signing on for the whole series and so on). Conversion rates show the digital marketer the effectiveness of the intended conversion tool. See **Retention metrics**.

Cost per action   Actions may vary (see **Engagement metrics**) but the best use of this spend is to obtain sales.

Customer relationship management (CRM) platform Software that allows businesses to handle relationships with customers. The platform stores and updates contact information and records of interactions with sales prospects. Enterprise systems include Siebel, Microsoft Dynamics, Oracle, Salesforce and SAP.

Defined user action   The desired action taken by your target customer. This may be filling out a web form, answering an email call to action, clicking on a link in a blog or any number of social media platform-dependent actions (liking on Facebook, retweeting on Twitter, following on Instagram and so on). See **Engagement metrics**.

Earned reach   Company-generated marketing assets across media channels that result in an increase in sharing of content, social mentions, reviews or followers.

Engagement metrics   Engagement metrics define what users do after encountering your marketing collateral. For example, after your marketing campaign, you should look to see if your potential customers interacted with your website, your brand's mobile app or your new interactive infographic. Check to see if they interacted with your Facebook content and, if so, did they like it? Did they follow your online advertisement to its landing page? Did they click on the button to order your product?

There are other metrics to measure for engagement detailed below:

- active users (daily or monthly);
- click-through rate or call to action effectiveness;

- defined user action;
- game or contest entrants;
- online chats or online seminar attendance;
- sharing and approval.

Game or contest entrants An online campaign may make use of games or contests to attract new customers or to familiarise them with a brand.

A digital marketer may create a promotion that relies on submission of contest entries or participation in an online game that extends over a period of time; successful contest entry or gameplay is another marker of engagement. Different social networks, such as Facebook, have specific rules about what constitutes a competition and how to market a competition to followers.

Impressions An impression is one view or display of an ad. Ad reports detail the total number of impressions per ad and are a relative measure of ad effectiveness. This refers to the instances where the digital marketer has a degree more certainty that the audience members saw the message due to its **reach**. For example, the website may have an audience of 3,000 people per day who come to the site. But the ad serving software recorded showing your advertisement upon page load only 300 times for those 3,000 visits. Likewise, if the ad serving platform had opted to show your ad twice to every visitor at the top and bottom of the page, then your impressions would be 6,000.

Inbound links (also known as incoming links, in-links or back links) These show the number and URLs of links on a web page that originate on another website. If the originating site is ranked more highly than your own website, then the links will carry more weight in website ranking terms.

Interactive Advertising Bureau (IAB) A consortium of 650 media and technology companies that sell, deliver or optimise advertising and marketing campaigns. The consortium works together to develop industry-wide technical standards and best practices as well as supporting research and education. See www.iab.com.

Market share   The company's percentage of the industry's total sales. This gives a measure of success and allows the company to adjust its marketing plan and cement its position in the market.

Media coverage   How many media channels are covering stories about your company. More media channels mean that more viewers will read news and **breadth reach** will increase.

Media Rating Council (MRC)[1]   A United States industry-funded organisation that accredits ratings services and allows auditing of broadcast ratings and measurement services.

Multi-channel marketing   Marketing to customers across a variety of channels.

Online chats, webinars or online seminar attendance   These are digital marketing measures of engagement and success. Participation in online 'events' such as chats or webinars allows a more dynamic and fluid interaction with the brand, while promoting conversation about the brand's intended topic. Chats – whether web chats, Twitter chats or even those mediated by a chatbot – tend to focus around a topic or theme. Online seminars are often intended to deliver educational or business value, related to the brand's expertise, and create goodwill. See **Engagement metrics**.

Organic reach   The extent to which customers have seen your marketing content or absorbed your message without cost to the business.

Page rank   Page rank is the result of which page the Google web search algorithm, among other search engine algorithms, ranks websites in its search results. Search engines look for several factors when ranking pages. If your web page has been updated frequently, has the most relevant, recent content and is appropriately titled and has Alt. tagged images, your page will appear high up in the search results, perhaps on page 1.

Page views A page view is a viewing of an instance of a page loaded on a browser. Repeated views of a single page are counted in this metric.

Paid reach The amount of people that you have paid to reach with your marketing.

Playbook In business, and especially in marketing, this is the documentation and plans that describe the actions that the business will take in order to achieve sales, marketing, advertising and other related business goals and targets.

Programmatic This term refers to an automated system that calculates the cost of an ad or marketing campaign in real time and adjusts pricing according to the popularity of the ad or advertising.

Quality score This is a score determined by services like Google and Facebook to influence the price they can charge for ad placement and revenue generation.

To determine the placement of ads, search engine bids – the price which the advertiser is prepared to pay for the ad – are multiplied by the quality score of the ad. Search engines do not disclose all the factors they include in calculating the quality score to protect their intellectual property, although factors such as click-through rate and landing page quality are included in the calculation. Better quality scores on web pages have a lower bid cost to the digital marketer and appear higher in ad listings.

Reach Reach is essentially what the audience for your marketing content is on an ideal day. This would include, for example, the website traffic numbers for a blog post, the total number of followers of a Twitter, Instagram or Facebook account or the subscriber numbers for an email newsletter or a podcast that has taken your advertising. Reach describes the best upper bounds of your campaign.

Reach is described in multiple ways depending on the nature of the campaign. Reach can be **earned** or viral (a social media personality praises your company without thought to payment for example, or a video created by a fan goes madly viral on YouTube) or **paid** (see **Quality score**) – the ad platform controls carefully the amount of exposure your marketing message has.

The following list shows examples of reach terms that digital marketers need to consider in campaigns:

- earned or viral or paid;
- impressions;
- lead generation;
- targeting or qualified reach.

Relationship management   This is simply the management of various business relationships. It can be as simple as a salesperson keeping in touch via mobile phone with a customer, or a multi-million-pound CRM system installed to keep a large corporation's business clients happy. For the digital marketer, their first marketing efforts in acquiring and maintaining engagement with customers should tie into their company's overall relationship management system. It would be ineffective to spend money gaining customers only to lose track of them. Engagement mechanisms such as blogs, social networking sites, email campaigns and online competitions are intended to help a company continue this good relationship with their customers once the digital marketer has started it. Each CRM platform evaluates relationship management differently but it is something the digital marketer needs to track and monitor.

Relationship management systems   These track the retention rate – the rate by which a company continues to retain customers (often subscribers) in the face of cancellations. This is a longer-term measure than **churn** or **bounce rate** because the earliest acquired (and retained) customers continue to age in the system.

Retention metrics   Marketers need to manage how many people stay on site – whilst analysing why they leave: these are retention metrics. A digital marketer, having created a customer base with intentions of growing that base, needs to take careful measure of how many customers are loyal and how many seek the service or goods elsewhere after buying with their company. These metrics are particularly important to businesses that expect to have their customers upgrade or trade in the product, for continued services like hairstylists or mechanics or for subscription models where the customer pays a monthly fee. Because these measures are as varied and unique to each business as they can be, it is best to start with basic metrics and then adjust to the business need.

Return on investment (ROI)   A calculation of the value of the return – whether a financial uplift or sentiment change – compared to the cost of the investment. Usually measured as:

$$\text{ROI (percentage)} = \frac{\text{Results of financial efforts}}{\text{Cost of efforts}}$$

Return on marketing investment (ROMI)   An overall assessment on marketing campaigns, giving a meaningful measurement of marketing success across all channels and metrics. It is calculated as:

$$\frac{\text{Uplift (extra value provided – cost)}}{\text{Cost of marketing efforts}}$$

Search engine marketing (SEM)   Advertisement of the company's product, web presence, landing page or other marketing target at the top of search engine results.

Search engine optimisation (SEO)   Tuning one's business website such that when search engine crawlers encounter it, they can easily parse the site's hierarchy of information and place it higher in search results.

Sentiment analysis   This is a technical term where natural language software or speech or facial recognition software can figure out how customers are feeling or reacting to a stimulus (online content, in-person content). Nielsen Consumer Neuroscience uses biometrics, eye-tracking and facial coding to analyse consumer online behaviour. As this book goes to press, several start-up companies exist, such as Palo Alto-based Sighthound and Emotient in the United States, and Swiss-based nViso, that study facial response to marketing messages and offer analysis to the companies who created the marketing. As sentiment analysis advances in both online mediums and in person, it will prove a valuable marketing tool. Social networking platforms such as Facebook now have a range of 'Reactions' that customers can select to give digital marketers a much clearer insight into how customers feel about content. See **Dissatisfaction analysis**.

Server-side ad insertion   Also called 'ad stitching' among video ad industry members, this is the technology that allows video ad content and video content to be stitched together from two diverse sources. Usually videos are served from content delivery networks (CDNs) and the ads come from elsewhere – this combination in the back-end technologies allows a seamless experience for the viewer and ensures that ad-blocking technologies on browsers or devices do not prevent the ad play.

Sharing   The count of all the instances where your content was made available to others by users of a social platform. This is measured differently based on the platform (retweets for Twitter, shares for Facebook and other sites). The market industry standard Net Promoter score is based on this key question: 'Would you recommend this product or service to a friend?' and a share means exactly that. The customer on this occasion has become the brand's advocate. Usually the social platform has its own methods of counting these shares and the digital marketer will track them. See **Engagement metrics**.

Social interactions   Measurement of the different types of interactions across social platforms your content has received over a specific period of time. Increasing the quality of social interactions across your networks will bring increased rapport with your customers. Conversely, inadequate quality, offensive content or content presented too often will cause follower churn.

Social media marketing (SMM)   Using a range of social media platforms and channels to market and measure marketing success across the brand's products and services.

Social platform   Software systems designed to promote or share content from users.

Sponsored content   Relevant content that has been paid for, either through payment to the host or influencer or by giving the product or service to be reviewed for free. Sponsored content must be clearly marked as such by bloggers or social media influencers in the US.

Statements of work (SOW)   Are descriptions of the work to be performed by the vendor. These will include project deadlines, descriptions of technology, expected sign off or review dates by the client, hardware or software licensing costs – in short, everything that the creative or marketing agency will do to fulfil the company requirements listed in the RFP.

Subscribers   How many people receive regular updates from your mailshots, blog or website. In the UK, these customers would have explicitly opted-in to receive your content. The General Data Protection Regulation (GDPR) ensures all subscribers keep full control over their data. All companies across the European Union (EU) must fully comply.

Targeting or qualified reach   This is a marketer's use of demographics to reach their target audience, the way Facebook, for example, allows targeted ads within its platform based on user profile or communities that represent a particularly friendly market for other reasons (affinity groups). See **Reach**.

Tweetstorm   A flurry of Twitter posts about a topic, or response to a controversial or newsworthy tweet.

User experience (UX)   Often confused with User Interface (UI), UX encompasses the entirety of what the user encounters. So, this includes content and the information hierarchy presented to the user, as well as how the business treats the customer in addition to the technical experience (refunds, customer support and so on).

Video advertising or ads   This is video content, usually run before a piece of content the user intends to watch. A glossary of video advertising terms is available from: http://dvglossary. www2.iab.com/.

NOTES

CHAPTER 1

1. Godin, S. (1999) *Permission Marketing: Turning Strangers into Friends, and Friends into Customers*. New York: Simon & Schuster.

CHAPTER 2

1. See www.smartinsights.com/digital-marketing-strategy/digital-strategy-development/10-reasons-for-digital-marketing-strategy/.

2. See https://www.internetlivestats.com/internet-users/.

3. See this example of how a Fitbit has been used to investigate a death: http://edition.cnn.com/2017/04/25/us/fitbit-womans-death-investigation-trnd/.

4. See https://www.facebook.com/business/learn/facebook-creative-tips-for-mobile-videos-ads.

5. See http://people.com/celebrity/all-by-myself-richard-dunn-makes-music-video-in-las-vegas/.

6. See https://www.goldmansachs.com/our-thinking/pages/virtual-and-augmented-reality-report.html.

7. See https://financesonline.com/top-5-crm-software-small-business-2017/.

8. See http://uk.pcmag.com/cloud-services/71221/guide/the-best-social-media-management-analytics-tools-of-2017.

9. See https://www.comscore.com/.

10. See https://www.pcmag.com/business/directory/social-media-analytics.

11. See https://blog.twitter.com/marketing/en_us/a/2016/new-research-tv-viewers-who-engage-on-twitter-have-higher-rates-of-ad-recall.html.

12. See https://www.gov.uk/marketing-advertising-law/direct-marketing.

13. See https://www.tpsonline.org.uk/.

14. See https://www.fpsonline.org.uk//fps/.

15. See https://corporate.mpsonline.org.uk/.

16. See http://app.leg.wa.gov/RCW/default.aspx?cite=19.190.

17. See https://www.prospects.ac.uk/job-profiles/digital-marketer.

18. See https://www.youtube.com/tarahunt.

19. Brogan, C. (2010) *Social Media 101*. Hoboken, NJ: John Wiley & Sons.

20. See this study on Costco and its free samples: Pinsker, J. (1 October 2014) "The psychology behind Costco's free samples." *The Atlantic*. Available from https://www.theatlantic.com/business/archive/2014/10/the-psychology-behind-costcos-free-samples/380969/.

21. See https://venngage.com/blog/visual-content-marketing-statistics.

22. See https://www.cisco.com/c/en/us/solutions/collateral/service-provider/visual-networking-index-vni/complete-white-paper-c11-481360.html.

23. See https://blog.hubspot.com/marketing/video-marketing-statistics.

24. See https://www.entrepreneur.com/article/248334.

25. See https://www.edwardtufte.com/tufte/.

26. See https://www.salon.com/2017/07/24/kid-friendly-emoji-movie-parodies-the-handmaids-tale-in-jarringly-insensitive-tweet/.

27. See http://newsroom.fb.com/news/2016/03/news-feed-fyi-taking-into-account-live-video-when-ranking-feed/.

28. See https://www.garyvaynerchuk.com/biography/.

29. See http://willitblend.com/.

30. See https://www.theglobeandmail.com/life/health-and-fitness/fitness/leah-mclaren-paleo-crossfit-and-the-art-of-joyless-living-health/article34111585/.

31. See https://www.w3.org/.

32. See https://www.bing.com/toolbox/webmaster.

33. See https://www.google.com/webmasters/.

34. See https://marketinglandevents.com/smx/london/.

35. See https://www.brightonseo.com/.

36. See https://www.internationalsearchsummit.com/london.html.

37. See http://sascon.co.uk/.

38. https://marketinglandevents.com/smx/london/.

39. See https://www.searchcamp.co.uk/.

40. See https://www.slideshare.net/.

41. See https://www.sprinklr.com/the-way/.

42. See http://sproutsocial.com/insights/social-media-best-practices/.

43. See https://hootsuite.com/education.

44. See https://Mashable.com.

45. See www.adweek.com/.

46. See https://techcrunch.com/social/.

47. See www.huffingtonpost.com/news/social-media/.

48. See www.cnbc.com/social-media/.

49. See https://dma.org.uk/training.

50. See http://the-cma.com/research/cma-industry-reports/industry-report-two/.

51. See https://iabuk.net/.

52. See www.mmaglobal.com/local-council/united-kingdom.

CHAPTER 3

1. Carnegie, D. (1936) *How to Win Friends and Influence People.* New York: Simon and Schuster.

2. See https://www.sfia-online.org/en/framework/sfia-7.

3. See https://www.cim.co.uk/more/professional-marketing-competencies/.

4. See https://themasb.org/.

5. See https://www.ama.org.

6. See http://marketing-dictionary.org/ama.

7. See https://www.theiimp.org/internationally-accepted-marketing-standards/.

8. See https://www.nielsensocial.com/social-content-ratings-standardizes-social-tv-measurement-across-facebook-and-twitter/.

9. See https://www.gov.uk/marketing-advertising-law/direct-marketing.

10. See https://www.sas.com/en_us/insights/marketing/multichannel-marketing.html.

11. See https://mediadecoder.blogs.nytimes.com/2011/09/28/for-advertising-study-says-more-screens-are-better/?_r=0.

12. See https://www.mediapost.com/publications/article/197803/the-whole-story-media-double-acts.html.

13. See https://www.sparkol.com/engage/8-classic-storytelling-techniques-for-engaging-presentations/.

14. See https://edgylabs.com/2017/05/07/burger-king-google-home-amazon-echo/.

15. See https://www.mystatesman.com/news/local/dustup-over-wonder-woman-screenings-alamo-offers-men-free-dvds/qzOTuqhJ3gyZgZq6lfnOMN/.

16. See http://variety.com/2017/film/news/wonder-woman-box-office-worldwide-1202453379/.

17. See http://variety.com/2017/digital/news/wonder-woman-twitter-record-2017-1202457742/.

18. See http://variety.com/2017/film/news/baywatch-wonder-woman-social-media-buzz-1202440025/.

19. See https://www.theglobeandmail.com/arts/film/some-women-only-screenings-planned-for-wonder-woman/article35142009/.

20. See https://www.mystatesman.com/news/local/dustup-over-wonder-woman-screenings-alamo-offers-men-free-dvds/qzOTuqhJ3gyZgZq6lfnOMN/.

21. See https://www.wired.com/2013/02/oreo-twitter-super-bowl/.

22. See https://www.forbes.com/sites/jenniferrooney/2013/02/04/behind-the-scenes-of-oreos-real-time-super-bowl-slam-dunk.

23. See http://adage.com/article/special-report-super-bowl/eggo-turns-stranger-things-role-free-super-bowl-spot/307879/.

24. See https://www.youtube.com/watch?v=9Egf5U8xLo8.

25. See https://www.bbc.com/news/uk-england-36064659.

26. See https://www.nytimes.com/2016/03/22/world/europe/boaty-mcboatface-what-you-get-when-you-let-the-internet-decide.html.

27. See https://www.bbc.co.uk/news/uk-36225652.

28. See https://www.telegraph.co.uk/news/2017/05/16/mcdonalds-apologises-disgusting-tv-advert-upsets-viewers/.

29. See https://www.nytimes.com/2017/04/05/business/kendall-jenner-pepsi-ad.html.

30. See https://twitter.com/SouthernRailUK/status/884769193366867968.

31. See https://www.telegraph.co.uk/news/2017/07/13/southern-rail-passengers-face-misery-drivers-vote-strike-august.

32. See https://www.nytimes.com/2017/04/04/business/media/nivea-ad-online-uproar-racism.html.

33. See www.bbc.co.uk/news/uk-40047816.

CHAPTER 4

1. Dweck, C. S. (2007) *Mindset: The New Psychology of Success*. New York: Penguin Random House.

2. See https://www.linkedin.com/groups/54066/profile.

3. See https://www.linkedin.com/groups/6770439/profile.

4. See https://www.linkedin.com/company/16262.

5. See https://www.linkedin.com/groups/1780141/profile.

6. See http://cim.co.uk.

7. See https://cpduk.co.uk/.

GLOSSARY

1. See https://www.mediaratingcouncil.org/History.htm.

INDEX